Martín Güemes: TYRANT OR TOOL?

A Study of the Sources of Power of an Argentine Caudillo by

ROGER M. HAIGH

TEXAS CHRISTIAN UNIVERSITY MONOGRAPHS IN HISTORY AND CULTURE · No. 3 1968

Martín Güemes: TYRANT OR TOOL?

A Study of the Sources of Power of an

Argentine Caudillo

by

ROGER M. HAIGH

TEXAS CHRISTIAN UNIVERSITY PRESS, FORT WORTH

FIRST PRINTING
Copyright © 1968 by Texas Christian University Press

Library of Congress Catalogue Card No. 68-8359
Manufactured in the United States of America

To My Wife
Anne Mette

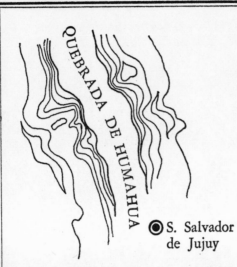

QUEBRADA DE HUMAHUA

◉ S. Salvador
   de Jujuy

● Campo Santo

◉ SALTA

● Cerrillos

ARGENTINA

● Est Castanares
   Guachipas

FOREWORD

For half a century after 1810 there was no national government in Argentina, except for brief intervals. The provinces were therefore independent; they did not secede, for there was nothing to secede from. Tyrannical caudillos or chieftains arose in these provinces to fill the political vacuum. These caudillos were usually self-appointed rulers whose followers were military rather than political. Some of them wielded great power, and they have frequently been referred to as absolute tyrants, as if there were no limits to their authority.

The purpose of this study is to analyze the rule and sources of power of one of the provincial caudillos, Martín Güemes of Salta. The analysis leads to a kinship elite of the leading landowning families, which dominated provincial affairs.

Familial relationships as bases for power structures have been studied before. Family structures were considered by Leonard Labaree, Carl Becker, and Carl Bridenbaugh in their analyses of political power in colonial America. Labaree examined each colony, and found all but New York and Massachusetts under the political and economic domination of aristocratic families.[1] Becker challenged the exclusion of New York, for he found political strife in that colony to be based solely on family feuding.[2] Bridenbaugh used a familial approach in his analysis of the colonial South..[3] And as early as 1789 David Ramsey was aware of the importance of family connections.[4]

In colonial Latin America there is ample evidence that Spanish authorities were aware of the power and potential of family structures. To prevent such groups from challenging royal authority, Spanish colonial laws prohibited royal officials from marrying into Creole families. Occasionally the king waived this rule, but only if the bride and groom were transferred to another territory.[5] In contrast to this legal attempt to limit family influence, both Church doctrine and land codes tightened the natural bonds of Creole families.[6]

On the local level the *cabildo* or town council has been described as "a closed corporation, membership purchased or inherited—passed around in rotation among the principal families of the town."[7] Municipal administration became the political instrument of wealthy Creole families.[8] In Latin American scholarship the family structure has usually been emphasized in general studies and overlooked in the particular.

John P. Gillin, in discussing the Spanish American family, described a rigid and patriarchal structure in which personal intimacy extended

v

through a much larger group of relatives than the modern American family. This structure weakened as industrialism and mobility increased, but it is still relatively strong.[9]

Gilberto Freyre considered the family to be the basic unit responsible for the successful colonization of Brazil. It was, he said, the main productive unit in the economy, and in politics it produced the most powerful aristocracy in the New World.[10] It not only held political control, but was able to limit the power of the Church.[11]

Frank Tannenbaum also emphasized the importance of the family in the development of what he called *compadrazgo* (spiritual relationship between a child's parents and the godfather) in his analysis of the functions of the *hacendado*. He viewed Latin American politics in terms of regional rivalries between regional families and regional caudillos.[12] The role of the individual was subordinated to his position within the family, which provided him with a basis for loyalty and political power.[13] The political power of the family was based on its size and on the prevalence of patriarchal elites. In the colonial era this power was expressed in family control of the local cabildos. Regional power was wielded by families through kinship ties with other ranking family elites, until extended families exerted power over vast regions.[14] Tannenbaum attributed the persistence of political, social, and economic regionalism to the survival of the influence of the local family.[15]

In specific investigations of the national period of Latin American history virtually no significance has been attached to family groups. This is surprising in light of the statements regarding the family by scholars such as Tannenbaum and Freyre.

I thank the Foreign Area Fellowship Program of the Ford Foundation for making it possible for me to visit Salta. There I was assisted greatly by Atilio Cornejo and Ramón Costello and his staff at the Archivo Histórico. Since this was the first time a North American had used this facility their courtesy was doubly appreciated.

The preparation of this study would have been difficult without the assistance of Donald E. Worcester of Texas Christian University, and Lyle N. McAlister of the University of Florida. By alternate encouragement and criticism they turned the author's ego into a badly battered one and in the process became as responsible as he is for whatever is good about this study.

Helpful suggestions were given by a number of individuals, including the late Arthur W. Thompson, David L. Dowd, and Francis Haber of the

University of Florida, Ronald C. Newton of Purdue University, W. T. Hagan of North Texas State University, and Alfred A. Cave of the University of Utah.

Finally, invaluable assistance came from a cheerful wife, Anne Mette, whose abilities in typing and editing were always helpful.

Fort Worth, Texas
June 1, 1968

ROGER M. HAIGH

FOOTNOTES (Foreword)

1. Leonard W. Labaree, *Conservatism in Early American History.* New York, 1948.
2. Carl L. Becker, *The History of Political Parties in the Province of New York, 1760-1776.* Madison, 1909.
3. Carl Bridenbaugh, *Myths and Realities: Societies of the Colonial South.* Baton Rouge, 1952.
4. Page Smith, *The Historian and History.* New York, 1964, p. 173.
5. Clarence H. Haring, *The Spanish Empire in America.* New York, 1947, p. 129.
6. José María Ots Capdequí, *El estado español en las Indias.* 2nd ed., México, 1946, pp. 73-77.
7. Haring, p. 153.
8. Ots Capdequí, p. 63.
9. John P. Gillin, "Some Signposts for Policy," in *Social Change in Latin America Today.* Ed. by Richard N. Adams. New York, 1960, pp. 33-34. See also Dwight B. Heath and Richard N. Adams, *Contemporary Cultures and Societies of Latin America.* New York, 1965, pp. 257-454.
10. Gilberto Freyre, *The Masters and the Slaves.* Transl. by Samuel Putnam. New York, 1946, p. 26.
11. *Ibid.,* p. 32.
12. Frank Tannenbaum, "Toward an Appreciation of Latin America," in *The U.S. and Latin America.* Englewood Cliffs, N.J., 1959, p. 15.
13. *Ibid.,* p. 37.
14. *Ibid.,* pp. 37-38.
15. *Ibid.,* pp. 15, 53.

CONTENTS

CONTENTS

CHAPTER I

Salta to 1815

The province of Salta occupies the northwestern region of Argentina. Physically, the region is dominated by a series of mountain chains running from north to south. These mountains are separated by fertile valleys and numerous rivers whose alluvial deposits regularly supplement the richness of the soil.[1] The proximity of the region to the tropic zone and the great variety in elevation give the area a spectrum of temperatures ranging from the subtropical valley floors to the frigid heights of the mountains. The greater part of the area is basically temperate.[2]

Such a variety of temperatures and elevations enables the region to produce a wide range of crops as long as there is sufficient rainfall. In the outlying areas the precipitation is too sparse to permit dry farming. Hence agriculture, and consequently most human activity, is concentrated in the central portion, the Valley of Lerma.[3] There the winter months see a heavy rainfall; so heavy, in fact, that during colonial times periodic floodings made transportation difficult.[4] The principal threats were the Río Grande de Jujuy, also known as the Río Bermejo, with its tributaries, the San Francisco and the Yavi; and the Río Pasaje and its tributaries, the Yataso, the Sali, and las Piedras.[5] Of these only the Bermejo was considered to be navigable, but it was exposed to attacks by hostile Indians.[6] The *salteños* chose to make the raising of livestock their main industry, and crops were cultivated only to provide winter feed. Basically, this pattern has remained unchanged.[7]

The difficult terrain was of military significance from 1810 to 1821. Three trails led from Salta to Upper Peru, but only one was practicable for the movement of an army. This trail, which went through the Quebrada de Humahuaca, was not passable by carts, and all military provisions and equipment had to be transported on the backs of men or mules.[8] This access difficulty made it virtually impossible for a sizable force to arrive in either Upper Peru or Salta with adequate provisions for an extended campaign. Also, the terrain made possible the attack on supply lines of either the Spanish or the patriots. This terrain proved to be Salta's best defensive ally in the period under examination, but it also served to prevent Argentina from controlling territories claimed in Upper Peru.

Salta's location made it an important trade center in the colonial period and contributed to its strategic military importance during the Wars of Independence. The city was founded in 1582 as a military post

1

to protect the trade route from Tucumán to Upper Peru.[9] It gradually acquired economic importance as well by selling supplies and mules to traders en route to the mining regions.[10] By 1750 Salta had become one of the major trade centers in Argentina.[11]

The advantageous location, combined with a temperate climate and a reasonably fertile soil, attracted a moderately large number of Spanish settlers. These families recognized the economic potential of the area and concentrated their efforts on raising mules and a variety of agricultural products that were in demand in Upper Peru.[12] The location of the province favored the mule industry, as Salta was the last point on the route from the coast to Upper Peru that could be reached by oxcart. In Salta cargoes had to be transferred to mules to manage the trails up into the Andes to destinations such as Potosí and Cuzco. By 1750 the salteños had established a virtual monopoly on the sale of the mules that were a basic necessity to the movement of goods in this portion of the Spanish Empire.

With profits obtained from the sale of mules and from commerce, Salta's economy became stable sooner than that of other parts of Argentina. Land was valued and *estancieros* acknowledged definite property lines.[13] The gauchos of Salta, unlike those of other parts of Argentina, were hired cowboys rather than lawless cattle-skinners. They lived on *estancias* and were loyal to the estancieros.[14] At the head of this socio-economic structure were the families that owned the land and controlled the commerce. Their role in the history of this era is all important.

Salta, city and province, grew in importance until the creation of the Viceroyalty of Río de la Plata in 1776, when commerce declined. The establishment of a royal treasury unit in Salta in 1778, and the city's role as the seat of an intendancy after 1792, added to the area's political importance.[15] A decline in the number of newcomers to the province simply served to entrench the land-owning Creole aristocracy more firmly in control. In 1810 the socio-economic conditions were stable, but the political importance of the area was imperceptibly declining.

In June, 1810, Salta and other provinces were asked to support the newly established junta of Buenos Aires. The royal governor of Salta, Nicolás Isamendi, called a *cabildo abierto,* a meeting of important citizens, which voted overwhelmingly to support the junta's right to rule the viceroyalty in the name of Ferdinand VII.[16] Fearing that the junta was leading the viceroyalty toward secession, Isamendi tried to maintain royalist control in Salta. Normally he would have called on the cabildo, but he knew that it was dominated by patriots.[17] Instead he sent a message to royalist General Vicente Nieto in Upper Peru. Nieto sent all of his salteño troops to Salta on leaves of absence. When they arrived Isamendi called another cabildo abierto, expecting the royalist soldiers to help him reverse the decision to support the junta of Buenos Aires.[18]

The plan failed, for José Antonio Fernández Cornejo persuaded the cabildo to exclude royalist soldiers from the cabildo abierto.[19] This open break between the cabildo and royalist officials widened when Isamendi arrested Cornejo and another cabildo member, Calixto Ruiz Gaona. A group of citizens protested this action, and Isamendi reacted by arresting Santiago Saravia, leader of the group. Public resentment mounted, and a mob freed the prisoners. Calixto Ruiz Gaona was sent to Buenos Aires for military aid. Worried by this popular action, Isamendi was completely discouraged when he learned that royalist authority had collapsed in the neighboring province of Córdoba.[20] He gave in, and Cornejo was appointed lieutenant governor.[21] When Ruiz Gaona returned with a military detachment and a new governor sent by the junta of Buenos Aires, he found the patriots in complete control. The new governor, Feliciano Chiclana, sent Isamendi to Buenos Aires as a prisoner.

With the creation of the Viceroyalty of Río de la Plata, Upper Peru (modern Bolivia) had been detached from Peru and attached to the new political unit. Upper Peru was the location of fabulous silver mines, and the Buenos Aires Junta was anxious to retain the province and its wealth. In October, 1810, General Antonio G. Balcarce reached Salta with an army on his way to Upper Peru. The city greeted Balcarce warmly and presented him with 10,000 pesos and a herd of mules, horses, and cattle.[22] Several companies of volunteers joined his troops on the march north.

After a minor defeat at Cotagaito,[23] Balcarce triumphed over the royalists at Suipacha.[24] Patriot rebels drove the royalists out of Cochabamba, and Upper Peru was under Balcarce's control. This was the crest of Buenos Aires' popularity in Upper Peru.[25] The tide soon ebbed.

The decline of porteño popularity began when Juan José Castelli, the civil administrator attached to Balcarce's army, began to establish a civilian administration. Castelli, ignoring the feelings of the people of Upper Peru, began a virtual reign of terror.[26] He drew up lists of suspects, confiscated property freely, and tried to replace Catholicism with the "Religion of Reason." He purged all town cabildos of anyone who did not support the new order with sufficient enthusiasm.[27] In 1812 the Archbishop of Charcas and the Bishops of La Paz and Salta joined in a

denunciation of the revolution.

3

denunciation of the revolution.[28] Castelli's actions were widely resented, and this resentment was turned against Buenos Aires.

Castelli crowned his errors by signing a truce with General José Manuel de Goyeneche, which enabled the royalist leader to reassemble his scattered forces and to recruit those disillusioned with the Argentines.[29] On June 20, 1811, Goyeneche broke the truce and crushed Balcarce's army at Huaqui. Only a diversion by patriots of Cochabamba distracted Goyeneche long enough for Balcarce to save part of his army.[30] In September the remnants of Balcarce's army straggled into Salta.

News of Castelli's actions in Upper Peru had already soured the salteños on Buenos Aires' administrative bungling. Balcarce's thorough defeat was an added disappointment to them. Thereafter when Buenos Aires sought salteño assistance for expeditions to Upper Peru, the response was unenthusiastic.

Goyeneche turned back another Argentine force at Suipacha in January, 1812, and the Army of the North was reduced to less than regimental strength.[31] Buenos Aires' prestige in Salta reached its nadir. When in March, 1812, General Manuel Belgrano arrived to take command of the military forces in the province, he had to restore the junta's prestige as well as rebuild a shattered army.

Belgrano reorganized the ordnance system, re-established discipline, and rearmed his forces.[32] He reassembled the cabildo and dissolved the provincial junta, paid for military supplies purchased locally, and recommended that the central junta not only act less arbitrarily but also consider local feelings in local affairs.[33] Belgrano's policies were favorably received in Salta, and he soon found local support stronger and recruitment easier. His relations with the Church offset these successes somewhat, for his attempts to arrest the royalist Bishop of Salta, Nicolás Videla, were for a time frustrated by salteños. But on July 1 Videla was arrested and sent to Buenos Aires.[34] His arrest was resented in Salta.

By July Belgrano was forced to cut short his program of military reorganization to face a military threat. Royalist forces under General Pío Tristán were beginning an offensive against patriot positions in northwest Argentina. With an army of only 1500 men Belgrano was forced to retreat.[35] Although under orders from Buenos Aires to evacuate Salta and Tucumán, Belgrano chose to disregard these instructions and to make a stand at Tucumán. On July 14, 1812, he issued a decree designed to force the salteños to emigrate south to Tucumán with all goods, livestock, and other valuable items from the province, thus presenting to the invading royalists an area of desolation. All who failed to obey this decree were to be treated as traitors.[37] The cabildos of Salta and Jujuy protested immediately, but their protests were ignored, and on August 23 the retreat from the province began.[38]

Owing to pressure from the royalist vanguard, the patriots under Belgrano were not able to burn everything of value, and destruction was limited to the path of the army. Royalist forces occupied Salta in early September and pushed south to Tucumán, where they were turned back by Belgrano on September 22.[39] They fell back to Salta, where on February 18, 1813, Belgrano attacked them. The royalists surrendered and were allowed to return to Upper Peru without their arms and equipment.[40]

The invasion of 1812 and the corresponding evacuation of the province had produced several changes in the affairs of the region. The invasion had served to awaken Salta to the crudities of war but it had also altered the composition of power. Many of the people who participated in the evacuation to Tucumán transferred their economic interests elsewhere and did not return to Salta. Also, many families of deep-seated royalist sympathies, such as the Aramburus and the Castros, left the province with the royalist army.[41] The remaining citizens consisted of those whose basic way of life was irrevocably tied to the region, whether under the royalists or the patriots.

In May, 1813, Belgrano again invaded Upper Peru. Successive defeats by the royalist commander, Joaquín Pezuela, at Vilcapugio in October and Ayohuma in November, forced Belgrano into a disorganized flight from Upper Peru.

When he arrived in Jujuy Belgrano had less than 800 men. The city welcomed him, and 1,500 volunteers came from Salta to augment his forces.[42] Such a warm welcome even in retreat contrasted greatly with the apathy he had met in 1812. Part of the explanation for this change was the result of the evacuation of 1812 and the Tristán invasion, but another cause was the purge of all the suspected royalist sympathizers from Salta in 1813.

The purge of royalists originated in the cabildo in November, 1813, which presented Governor Feliciano Chiclana with a list of suspected royalists and the recommendation that they be banished. Chiclana agreed, and those on the list were forced to dispose of their property and emigrate. There was no trial, and it is likely that injustices occurred and that innocent people lost their homes in the enforcement of the action.[43] This stern measure committed the province thoroughly to the patriot cause, and partially explains the enthusiastic support that Belgrano received after his retreat from Upper Peru.

Belgrano, despite the support he received from Salta, chose to evacuate the province rather than face the invading royalists under Pezuela. The people withdrew to the southern edge of the province.[44] There the salteños under Pedro José Saravia and other estancieros began grouping themselves into guerrilla bands to resist the royalist advance on Tucumán. This was the beginning of the tremendous resistance to the royalists which earned for Salta the title "Bulwark of the North."

Belgrano completed his retreat to Tucumán, and the royalists occupied Salta without serious resistance. In January General José de San Martín replaced Belgrano in Tucumán, and he sent Martín Güemes to Salta to take charge of irregular resistance.[45] By the time Güemes arrived the estancieros had already organized very effective resistance. Among the larger groups of salteño gauchos were those under the command of Apolinar Saravia, Luis Burla, Pedro José Zavala, and José Francisco Gorriti. These units introduced the royalists to a new form of warfare, the wild, pell-mell charges of the gaucho cavalry, the stealthy night attacks, and the constant harassment of lines of communication and supply.

The immediate aim of the salteño resistance was to cut the Spanish forces off from any source of supply of cattle and horses. At first weapons of the gauchos were mainly lances and *bolas,* but after they captured large quantities of arms from the enemy they became among the best armed soldiers of the times.[47] They used cavalry exclusively, and hit and run tactics were the most common forms of combat. The raiders would fall on a column of enemy troops as often as twelve times a day, and they frequently stampeded herds of horses through the royalist ranks or set fire to the grass. If the Spanish force was small enough, it would be totally destroyed.[48] Since both sides killed their prisoners, surrender was no guarantee of safety.[49]

By March the royalists knew that small foraging parties sent out of the city in search of meat and horses would be destroyed. As a result only large expeditions were sent. But even these large forces might be attacked simultaneously by several bands of salteños. For example, on March 29 Güemes and Gorriti destroyed a royalist force of approximately 300 men. On May 27 Pezuela arrived with 3,200 reinforcements, and attempted to obtain supplies by sending two Spanish divisions south to sweep away resistance. Güemes defeated the first column on June 2, and Pedro Zavala pursued the second to the gates of Salta. In June Pezuela received the rumor that Montevideo had fallen to the patriots. Since his plan had been to link up with the royalists at Montevideo, the news discouraged him from any further attempts to penetrate the southern portion of the province and caused his retreat to the safety of Upper Peru.[51]

Under Pezuela terror had prevailed in Salta. Families which had not emigrated were subjected to all forms of abuse. Homes of people who had followed the patriots were destroyed, and the city was completely pillaged. Pezuela's actions gave the people of Salta an enduring hatred of royalist rule.[52]

The next few months brought confusion to the political and military situation in Salta. Politically, the policies of Buenos Aires caused irritation and disappointment. After the evacuation of Pezuela's forces, a new governor, Bernabé Aráoz, began a dispute with the cabildo. In October, 1814, the Buenos Aires government, with the support of Aráoz, divided the province of Salta. The southern portion, which had escaped looting by Pezuela, was transferred to the authority of Tucumán, and Salta retained jurisdiction over little more than a wasteland. The second area of conflict between the cabildo and Aráoz resulted from a tax of 2 per cent levied by the cabildo on all property held by Europeans. The purpose of the tax was to provide funds for the Army of the North, and its targets were the royalist merchants and landholders within the province. Aráoz opposed it, but the cabildo supported it. Aráoz appealed to Buenos Aires and was upheld. The tax was rejected, but not without the sacrifice of a great deal of porteño popularity in Salta. Aráoz resigned in November, 1814, and was replaced by Hilarión de la Quintana, a more popular figure, who held the governorship until 1815.[54]

Militarily, the situation was also confusing to the salteños. After the evacuation of Pezuela, the Army of the North under José Rondeau entered Salta and began preparations for another invasion of Upper Peru. In January, 1815, Montevideo fell and new reinforcements from Buenos Aires arrived in Salta. Most of these troops had participated in the siege of Montevideo. With the incorporation of Güemes and the gauchos of Salta into the army, hopes were high for a successful invasion of Upper Peru. Then news arrived that Rondeau was to be replaced by Carlos Alvear.[55] This caused a split in the army between devotees of Rondeau and Alvear. The Rondeau faction revolted and gained control of the Army of the North. Rondeau sent word that Alvear would not be accepted, and in so doing cut the Army of the North's ties with Buenos Aires.[56] Salteños were more concerned with the invasion of Upper Peru and the presence

7

of Rondeau's army than they were with maintaining loyalty to the unstable regime in Buenos Aires, and they joined Governor Quintana in denouncing the central government.

In March Rondeau invaded Upper Peru accompanied by Quintana, who left the post of governor of Salta to serve in the army.[57] On April 14 Rondeau defeated Pezuela at Puerto Grande del Marqués. Güemes and his gauchos played a key role in the victory.[58]

Immediately after the battle Güemes and 1,000 men returned to Salta. The reasons for this move are not completely clear, yet the reaching of a rapprochement between Alvear and Pezuela, and Güemes' conviction that the invasion would fail seem the most acceptable.[59] On the way to Salta Güemes stopped at Jujuy to seize 500 rifles from Rondeau's arsenal. He then proceeded to Salta, where he was enthusiastically received. He warned the salteños to prepare for Rondeau's defeat and another royalist invasion. At this juncture landowning aristocrats took matters into their own hands and on May 6, 1815, elected Güemes governor of the province.[60]

As has been noted from 1810 to 1815 Salta was under the jurisdiction of governors appointed by Buenos Aires. The actions of Buenos Aires, therefore, had a definite impact on the attitude of the salteños. Another factor that must be kept in mind is the nature of the breach with Spain in 1810. Although patriot leaders proclaimed that their actions were in the name of Ferdinand VII, their goal was independence. Pretended loyalty to Spain continued from 1810 to 1816. These facts must be remembered when one reviews the reactions to events, anticipated or accidental, that occurred during those times. On one hand there were some events that triggered reactions shared by all segments of the population. On the other hand some actions were of concern to only a particular group within the society.

Among the more general factors were: the execution of Santiago Liniers; the action of Castelli in Upper Peru; the rejection of the provincial deputies in 1811; the military defeats; the decree of Belgrano in 1812; the instability of government; the seeming lack of concern for the northwestern provinces; the division of the province of Salta; and some events of lesser importance.

The execution of Santiago Liniers took place soon after the movement away from Spain began. Liniers was the region's first national hero after he had successfully expelled the English in 1807. In 1810 Liniers associated himself with the ill-fated royalist junta in Córdoba. When the junta fell he was captured and executed without trial. This action shocked the salteños and marked the beginning of a sharp distrust of the porteños.[61]

This distrust was greatly stimulated by Castelli's terroristic acts during Balcarce's occupation of Upper Peru. These actions were sharply criticized because the Jacobinism of Castelli was not acceptable to the majority of the people, and he assumed powers that salteños felt were not his. When news of his blunders in Upper Peru circulated in Salta, Castelli found very few defenders.[62] It is clear that he did more lasting damage to the image of Buenos Aires than any other single individual.

Another cause for irritation against Buenos Aires was the rejection of the provincial deputies in 1812. The deputies, Juan Ignacio Gorriti and Francisco de Gurrachaga, were summarily dismissed and sent back to their provinces, Jujuy and Salta. Usurpation of absolute authority by Buenos Aires caused the salteños to question the essential difference between rule by Spain and rule by Buenos Aires.[63] Rejection of the deputies was a serious mistake, because it aggravated the disunion which plagued Argentina for half a century.

Balcarce's and Belgrano's defeats discredited Buenos Aires in the eyes of the salteños. Their forces marched through the provinces, recruited men and resources, and then proceeded to anticipated victories over the royalists. Months passed, and reports were received of victories at Huaqui, Vilcapugio, or Ayohuma. Then, inevitably, the army returned in flight. The reaction of the salteños was one of anger and disappointment, anger at the leaders, and disappointment at the defeats.

Belgrano's defeat in 1812 was the most irritating to the salteños, for Belgrano ordered them to leave the province with all of their valued possessions. The military wisdom of Belgrano's decree was apparent only later, but the evacuation gave salteños a first hand knowledge of the sacrifices of war. The general belief that Belgrano's defeat was the product of thoughtless acts by the porteños intensified salteño resentment against Buenos Aires.

The failure of the porteños to establish a stable government was another cause of irritation, for the exposed salteños often had to fight for their homes. The instability of the government of Buenos Aires repelled them.[64] It also colored the attitude of the provincial government toward Spain. Until 1814 the general trend was away from allegiance to Ferdinand VII, but after his return to Spain many men felt that the fighting should end. When it was rumored that Buenos Aires had entered negotiations with Ferdinand, many salteños felt betrayed.

The sense of betrayal was intensified by the seeming unconcern of Buenos Aires for the welfare of the northwestern provinces. Armies defeated in Upper Peru were pulled all the way back to Tucumán to make a stand against the royalists, and the provinces of Salta and Jujuy were left undefended. Tristán's brief invasion was not disastrous, but that of Pezuela cost the salteños much valuable property.[65] In this last invasion the irregular gaucho forces proved to be the most effective check on royalist aggression.

Finally, the salteños were angered by the division of their province in October, 1814, since this lessened their importance. It also ended the possibility of receiving economic support from Tucumán in the recovery of Upper Peru.[66] These acts contributed to the apathy that Belgrano described, and they explain Salta's disenchantment with Buenos Aires.

NOTES

1. Félix Best, *Historia de las guerras argentinas*. Buenos Aires, 1960, I, 59.
2. *Ibid.*, p. 60.
3. *Ibid.*, p. 61.
4. Preston James, *Latin America*. 1st ed. rev., New York, 1951, p. 271.
5. Best, I, 61.
6. "Reply of Pacheco to Juan Adrián Cornejo, August 33, 1778," in Atilio Cornejo, *Apuntes históricos sobre Salta*. 2d ed., Buenos Aires, 1937, pp. 427-429. Hereafter cited as Cornejo, *Apuntes*.
7. James, p. 271.
8. Best, I, 64.
9. "Act of the foundation of the city of Salta, April 16, 1582," in Cornejo, *Apuntes*, p. 108.
10. Bernardo Frías, *Historia del General D. Martín Güemes y de la Provincia de Salta de 1810 a 1832*. Salta, 1902, I, 63. See also Sir Woodbine Parrish, *Buenos Ayres and the Provinces of the Rio de la Plata. . . .* London, 1838.
11. Frías, I, 63.
12. *Ibid.*, p. 61.
13. This was affirmed by the careful delineation of property boundaries in the will and testament of Juan Adrián Fernández Cornejo, in Cornejo, *Apuntes*, p. 145. See also "Last will and testament of Gabriel de Güemes Montero," in Atilio Cornejo, *Historia de Güemes*, Buenos Aires, 1946, p. 16. Hereafter cited as Cornejo, *Historia*.
14. Frías, I, 87-97.
15. Cornejo, *Historia*, p. 13. Vicente D. Sierra, *Historia de la Argentina, 1810-1913*, Buenos Aires, 1962, V, 85-86. There was a schism in Salta society dating from 1807 when the Intendant Rafael de la Luz was replaced. Most of the pro-Luz faction were royalists who left Salta before 1813.
16. "Act of recognition of the Junta of Buenos Aires, June 26, 1810," in Cornejo, *Apuntes*, pp. 601-604.
17. Frías, I, 382-386.
18. *Ibid.*, p. 407.

19. "Letter of Feliciano Antonio Chiclana to the Junta of Buenos Aires, 9-1, 1810," in Cornejo, *Historia*, pp. 61-62.
20. Frías, I, 408-414.
21. Antonio Zinny, *Historia de los gobernadores de las provincias argentinas.* Buenos Aires, 1916-1921, V, 30.
22. Cornejo, *Historia*, pp. 75-76.
23. "Letter of Dr. Juan José Castelli to the Junta of Buenos Aires, Nov. 2, 1810," *Partes oficiales y documentos relativos a la Guerra de la Independencia Argentina: Archivo General de la Nación.* Buenos Aires, 1900, I, 32-33. Hereafter cited as *Partes oficiales.*
24. "Letter of Juan José Castelli to the Junta of Buenos Aires Nov. 2, 1810," *ibid.*, pp. 36-37.
25. *Memorias de Dámaso de Uriburu: 1794-1857.* Buenos Aires, 1934, p. 37. Hereafter cited as *Uriburu.*
26. *Ibid.*
27. Frías, II, 183-228.
28. *Ibid.*, p. 448.
29. *Uriburu*, p. 49.
30. "Report of Juan José Viamonte to Antonio Gonzales Balcarce, July 18, 1811," *Partes oficiales*, I, 125-126. See also *Uriburu*, p. 55.
31. Frías, II, 419.
32. "Letter of Manuel Belgrano to the Junta of Buenos Aires, January 17, 1812," *Documentos del Archivo de Belgrano*, Buenos Aires, 1914, IV, 62-63. Hereafter cited as *DAB.*
33. "Letter of Manuel Belgrano to the Junta of Buenos Aires, January 20, 1812," *ibid.*, p. 64.
34. "Letter of Belgrano to the Junta of Buenos Aires, March 13, 1812," *ibid.*, pp. 107-108. See also Frías, II, 481.
35. *Memorias póstumas de General José María Paz*, (Biblioteca Ayacucho, No. 16), Madrid, Editorial-America, n.d., p. 62. Hereafter cited as *Paz.*
36. Frías, II, 504.
37. "Decree of Belgrano to the citizens of Jujuy and Salta, July 14, 1812," *DAB*, IV, 107-172.
38. Frías, II, 511-512. See also *Paz*, p. 62.
39. "Letter of Belgrano to the Junta of Buenos Aires, Sept. 4, 1812," *Partes oficiales*, I, 181-185. See also *Uriburu*, p. 65.
40. *Paz*, pp. 133-134.
41. *Uriburu*, p. 86. In many cases the royalist group corresponded to the pro-Isamendi faction in the dispute of 1807.
42. Frías, III, 98.
43. *Uriburu*, p. 97.
44. *Paz*, p. 225.
45. *Ibid.*, p. 229.
46. *Uriburu*, pp. 91-92.
47. *Ibid.*, p. 104.
48. Best, I, 121.
49. *Uriburu*, p. 163.
50. *Ibid.*, p. 104.
51. Frías, III, 122-124.
52. *Uriburu*, p. 105.
53. Cornejo, *Historia*, p. 118.

11

54. Zinny, V, 48. See also Cornejo, *Historia,* pp. 118-120.
55. Ricardo Levene, *A History of Argentina* ("The Inter-American Historical Series"), ed. and transl. by James A. Robertson, Chapel Hill, 1937, p. 289.
56. *Paz,* p. 243.
57. Zinny, V, pp. 49-50.
58. *Paz,* pp. 267-269; See also *Uriburu,* p. 129.
59. This is fully discussed in Cornejo, *Historia,* pp. 126-128.
60. *Paz,* p. 136.
61. *Uriburu,* p. 30.
62. "Letter of Cornelio de Saavedra to Feliciano Antonio Chiclana, February 11, 1811," *DAB,* XII, No. 33, pp. 39-40.
63. "Letter of Belgrano to the Junta of Buenos Aires, July 28, 1812," *DAB,* IV, 179.
64. *Ibid.,* p. 180.
65. *Uriburu,* p. 105.
66. Cornejo, *Historia,* p. 118.

CHAPTER II

The Composition and Influence of The Kinship Elite, 1810-1815

The province of Salta was involved in war with the royalists of Upper Peru from 1810 to 1821. Documents concerning the raising of troops and funds for military supplies make frequent references to several prominent families: the Figueroas, Cornejos, Saravias, and Toledos, who enthusiastically supported the cause of independence.[1] These families owned or controlled a large part of the wealth, and they were related to the other families that controlled the remainder. These kinship connections were strengthened by isolation and by economic interests common to all. The four families composed the kinship elite. They and the families related to them dominated the province of Salta.[2]

The Spanish American family was close-knit by custom, and it was strengthened by legal code and religious doctrine. There were laws concerning dowries, estates, primogeniture, and the care of orphaned and adopted children,[3] which gave the family legal rights and duties. Through the Sacraments the Church gave the family strong spiritual ties.

In regions such as Salta, which were isolated and of difficult access, families had few outside distractions. They concentrated their interests on the locality, and all shared the same outlook. Those living in the large fertile valleys had the same economic problems and interests as their neighbors. The Figueroas owned one-fourth of the Valley of the Lerma, an area of about 80 square miles in the southwestern part of the province.[4] All of the many members of this powerful family were involved in the raising of cattle, horses, and mules.

The city of Salta had about 7,000 inhabitants, and the province about five times that number.[5] Since the population was small and the rate of growth stable, a few generations of intermarriages produced wide circles of relatives. The leaders of the most important families enjoyed a powerful influence simply through family connections.

In 1810 the Junta of Buenos Aires sent Feliciano Antonio Chiclana to Salta. Part of his mission was to report on the sources of patriot support. On September 1, 1810, he cited the Figueroas, Cornejos, and Gaonas as having given great aid to the cause of independence.[6] In his instructions to his successor on December 17, he called the Figueroas, Cornejos, and Saravias true patriots. Later he mentioned Vicente Toledo,

13

Domingo Puch, Lorenzo Mollinedo, and Gerónimo López as having rendered valuable assistance.[7]

The Figueroas were wealthy estancieros. Their landholdings ran from about nine miles southwest of Salta to about fifty miles south.[8] The name Figueroa appears frequently in lists of colonial cabildos. Their colonial station was shown by the fact that they were one of the five families that donated funds to set up a royal treasury in Salta in 1778.[9] Their basic source of wealth seems to have been cattle and mules, for they were one of the families mentioned by Frías as having profited greatly by the mule trade.[10] Some indication of the Figueroas' wealth was demonstrated in 1810. That year they donated over 22,000 pesos in silver to support the cause of independence.[11]

The military strength of the Figueroas was revealed at times of the Spanish invasions of the province. José Félix and Apolinar Figueroa led bands of gauchos into combat.[12] The family did not engage in the regular military organization of the province, but fought only when it was threatened. In times of peace the gauchos returned to the Figueroa estancias, reappearing only when enemy troops approached. The numerical strength of the forces controlled by the Figueroas was irregular, but in 1814 they personally raised two companies or upwards of 500 men.[13]

The second family of the kinship elite was that of the Cornejos. They were much like the Figueroas in economic position and social status. The center of Cornejo holdings was at San Isidora, northeast of Salta, where they owned several large estancias devoted to the raising of mules and cattle. The Cornejos were also engaged in the production of sugar.[14] Like the Figueroas, the Cornejos were members of the colonial Creole aristocracy of Salta. They were also one of the families that donated funds for the establishment of the royal treasury in Salta, and they were often represented in the cabildo.[15] Juan Adrián Fernández Cornejo was the central figure in the attempts to open the Río Bermejo to navigation.[16] When he died, he left 332,000 pesos worth of properties to be divided among his heirs. This figure excluded the home estancia of Campo Santo.[17]

Part of the Cornejos' support of the patriot cause was in the form of donations of livestock, but they were most important because of military manpower at their disposal. Their principal military leader was José Antonio Cornejo. He rose from commander of about 1,000 gauchos in 1810 to Commandant of the Province of Salta in 1821.[18] Francisco María Cornejo was a division commander from 1814 to 1821, and other family members held military rank from time to time. The wealth of the Cornejos was comparable to that of the Figueroas and the position of the

Cornejos in the military and political organizations of the province justified their inclusion in the kinship elite.

The third family mentioned by Chiclana was the Saravias. Again there was a marked similarity between the economic interests of the Saravias and those of the Figueroas and the Cornejos. The Saravias did not seem to have great stature throughout the colonial period, but the marriage of Pedro José Saravia to Bárbara Tineo provided this family with an entree into the kinship elite. Bárbara Tineo was one of three daughters in a family which owned the entire Valley of Lerma from Salta to Jujuy. On her father's death his holdings were split between the two married daughters and thus the Saravias became one of the largest landowning families in the province. (The other Tineo daughter married Domingo Sola and the third never married.) This division occurred in the 1780's. Shortly thereafter Pedro José Saravia was accepted as a Caballero of Charles III.[19] From 1810 to the fall of Güemes in 1821 they supported the patriot cause unstintingly. The family members were estancieros, and they aided the cause by providing supplies and gaucho troops.

During the pre-Güemes period the principal representative of Saravia political interests was Pedro José Saravia. He was a member of the first Junta of Salta in 1810, and provisional governor in 1811 and 1812. In 1812 he donated over 5,000 head of cattle to Belgrano's army, and in 1814 he was the general commandant of the salteño uprising against Pezuela.[20] After he became less active, his family continued to be well represented in the Güemes period. Both Satúrnino and Apolinar Saravia held gaucho commands in the resistance of 1814, and they continued in this capacity throughout the administration of Güemes.[21] By 1819 Apolinar was Chief of Staff of the military forces of Salta,[22] and in 1821 he led the salteño forces in defense of the province in the south after their defeat at Tucumán.[23] In 1821 Satúrnino Saravia was elected governor by the cabildo that ousted Güemes. He was soon deposed, but returned to the governorship after the death of Güemes.[24] Other Saravias who held military positions were Mateo, commander of a militia unit in 1811,[25] and Domingo, who commanded a unit of gauchos in 1814. The Saravias generally held at least three separate military commands throughout the period and were well represented politically.

The Toledos were the only family included in the kinship elite that Chiclana did not praise highly, though he did mention Vicente Toledo as one who contributed generously to the cause of independence. The family was prominent in the colonial era and was among those that financed the establishment of the treasury in colonial Salta.[26] Its leaders were estancieros whose holdings ran from Yataso south of Salta to the boundary with Tucumán. In 1780 an inventory of property listed 17,000 mules.[27] After 1810 they supported the patriot cause, and in the next five years donated over 1,300 head of horses to the army.[28] They did not, however, wield as much political and military power as the other three families.

The inclusion of the Toledos in the kinship elite was due primarily to their social position. They were direct descendants of Viceroy Francisco de Toledo,[29] and were representative of the old aristocratic Creole families of Salta. Their influence in the independence period was a reflection of their social connections. Whenever a dignitary of the government of Buenos Aires came to Salta he resided at Yataso, the home of the Toledos. Among the prominent visitors during this period were Juan Martín de Pueyrredón, Manuel Belgrano, and José de San Martín.[30] Social connections with such powerful national figures gave the Toledos considerable influence.

The Toledos were closely connected to the Figueroas, for María de Toledo was the wife of Antonio de Figueroa, the patriarch of the Figueroa family.[31] This connection added to the importance of both families.

The connection between the Toledos and the Figueroas was indicative of the interconnections among the kinship elite and with other wealthy families of the region. Marriages were evidently contracted along economic lines. The rich married the rich and the poor married the poor.

The Figueroas and the Cornejos were particularly closely related. In two generations the Cornejos married into the Figueroa family five times.[32] Magdalena Cornejo, the daughter of Antonio F. Cornejo, married Francisco Javier Figueroa. Gabriela Goyechea, the daughter of María Ignacia Cornejo, married Narciso Figueroa. María Mercedes Cornejo, the sister of María Ignacia and daughter of Juan Adrián Cornejo, married Apolinar Figueroa. Cornelia Cornejo, daughter of José Antonio Cornejo, married Eugenio Figueroa. Melchora Figueroa, daughter of Narcisco Figueroa, married Gregorio A. Cornejo. These connections were illustrative of mutual interests.[33]

Also illustrative of the clannishness of these families was the high incidence of marriages within them. Not only did the Figueroas, for example, marry into related families such as the Cornejos, but marriages were frequent among first cousins within the families. Mercedes Figueroa married Mariano Figueroa Aráoz. The father of the bride and the father of the groom were brothers. The same situation occurred in the marriage of Damasena Figueroa to José Figueroa Güemes.[34]

16

The fourth family, the Saravias, was not closely tied into the kinship elite.[35] The direct connection was limited to the marriage of Juan José Saravia to María Cornejo, the daughter of José Antonio Cornejo.[36] However, the kinship connection was solidified by connections to other families related to the Figueroas, Cornejos, and Toledos. The most obvious example of this secondary relationship was the linkage of all four families in the kinship elite to the Castellanos.[37]

As a result of marriage, the kinship elite was directly related to the following families during the period under scrutiny: Burla, Alvarado, Mollinedo, Castellanos, Güemes, Ibazeta, Murua, Ovejero, Otaso, Costas, Ceballos, Matorras, San Millán, Fernández, Arias, Paz, Cruz Monge, Arenales, De la Corte, Medeiros, Usandivares, Goyechea, Femayor, Heredia, Latorre, Aráoz, Valdés, López, Lozcano, Boedo, Torino, Pardo, Falcón, Plazaola, Ormaechea, Tineo, Ancieta, Aguirre, and Jáurequi.[38] If the average membership of a family is assumed to be approximately fifty members, these families would make up a group of about 2,000 people, or about 5 per cent of the population of the province of Salta. This network of families, headed by the kinship elite, controlled the socio-economic power of the region.

The two richest families of the colonial era, the Gurrachagas and Moldes, were not represented in the structure. While both of these families were connected secondarily to the kinship elite, the nature and the extent of their wealth made them less important from 1810 to 1821 than they had been in the late colonial period.

Both families were basically merchants with interprovincial interests. When Belgrano ordered the province stripped of everything of value in 1812, the families of Gurrachaga and Moldes transferred their main commercial interests out of Salta.[39] The only representative of the former family who remained active in the affairs of Salta was José de Gurrachaga. The role of the latter family was limited to the activity of Eusebio and José Moldes. Both were in the national army, and both left Salta prior to 1814.[40]

The families making up the kinship elite had much in common. All were patriots, and all were deeply rooted in the area. While all were estancieros, all were directly related to families actively engaged in commerce.[41] Such connections with merchant families gave the members of the kinship elite an awareness of the interests of groups that were not primarily cattlemen. The possession of property and the traditional cooperation of the merchants and the estancieros in the trading of mules gave the kinship elite and related families a basis for economic solidarity.[42] In 1810 another unifying factor was added in the form of patriotism. Their ideas of nationality, however, were confined to what they knew and understood, Salta and the immediate environs of the province. Beyond these geographic limits their concept of nationhood was vague and uncertain.

In 1810 Salta was faced with a decision as to whether it should recognize the junta in Buenos Aires or the one in Spain. The salteños chose to recognize Buenos Aires, and the royalist reaction was sudden and intense. The kinship elite and Salta found themselves committed to a struggle that threatened their existence. The first phase of this struggle was from 1810 to 1815.

The seat of political power becomes apparent when the connections of the individual members of the cabildos are examined. Such an examination shows that the kinship elite controlled an effective majority in the cabildo from 1810 to 1815.[43] The cabildo of 1810 was dominated by José Antonio Cornejo, a central figure in the history of Salta throughout the period. Other members who were related to the major families were Calixto Ruiz Gaona, Nicolás Arias Rengel, José Francisco Boedo, and Juan Antonio Murua. Calixto Ruiz Gaona's daughter married Luis Burla,[44] the brother of Inés and José Burla.[45] Nicolás Arias Rengel was directly related to Pedro Pablo Arias, Juan P. Arias, and Grimensa Arias, who married into the Saravia, Cornejo, and Figueroa families respectively.[46] José Francisco Boedo was directly connected to the kinship elite through the marriage of Tiburcio Cornejo to Ventura Boedo.[47] Juan Antonio Murua's son Miguel married into the Figueroa family.[48] In 1810 the first four families were thus represented by five of the seven cabildo members.[49]

In 1811 the cabildo was replaced by a Provisional Junta. The members of the Provisional Junta were all connected to the core families. Juan José Cornejo and Pedro José Saravia were members of it. Dr. Pedro Arias Velásquez and Juan Antonio Moldes were related to the Saravia family.[50] Francisco Aráoz was directly connected to both the Figueroas and the Cornejos.[51]

In 1812 the Provisional Junta was abolished and the cabildo re-established. Again the family structure commanded a majority of the seats.[52] It was represented by Fructuoso Figueroa. Álvarez de Arenales was related to the Figueroas through the marriage of Mercedes Arenales to Baltazar de Usandivares.[53] Gerónimo López was also connected to the Figueroas as Benita López married Alejandro Figueroa, José Luis López married Isabel Figueroa, and Maximiliano López married Dionisia Figueroa.[54] Ángel Alvarado was related to the Toledo family by the marriage of his brother Juan Francisco to Pastora Toledo.[55] Isidoro de Matorras was connected to both the Figueroas and the Cornejos, as Policarpo Matorras married Josefa Florentina Figueroa, the daughter of Francisco Javier Figueroa and Magdalena Cornejo.[56] The kinship elite thus held five of the eight seats in the cabildo.

In 1813 the cabildo was completely controlled by individuals related to the kinship elite.[57] Hermenegildo G. de Hoyos had a secondary connection to the Saravia family.[58] Mariano Boedo was related to the Cornejo family through the marriage of Tiburcio Cornejo to Ventura Boedo. Guillermo de Ormaechea was married to Rudecinda Saravia,[59] and his sister was married to Eusebio de Mollinedo of the Toledo family.[60] Severo de Alvarado was also directly affiliated with the Toledo family through his brother's marriage to Pastora Toledo.[61] The López family connection to the Figueroas has been traced, and José D. Fernández was related to both the Figueroas and the Cornejos through the marriage of Celedonio Fernández to Ventura Figueroa. Ventura was the daughter of Francisco Javier Figueroa and Magdalena Cornejo.[62]

The cabildo of 1814 was the last to function under the sole jurisdiction of a governor appointed by the central government in Buenos Aires. In this assembly the family structure was represented by four of the seven members.[63] Two of these four, Guillermo de Ormaechea and Gerónimo López, had held seats prior to 1814, and their relationship to the four families has been established. The other two were Juan de la Cruz Monge y Ortega and Gaspar Arias. The former married the daughter of María Antonia Figueroa and Francisco González de San Millán.[64] Gaspar Arias was related through family ties to the Saravias, the Figueroas, and the Cornejos.[65]

As a consequence of the domination of the cabildo by the kinship elite and the related families, the political power of this group was formidable. Despite the presence of an appointed governor, the cabildo was responsible for the administration of the province, the collection of taxes, and the material and financial support of the military forces. It should also be noted that the governor was frequently absent, and his replacements, such as Pedro José Saravia and José Antonio Cornejo, came from the family structure.

The manifestations of the military power of the kinship elite from 1810 to 1815 can be divided into two phases. The first phase covers the period from 1810 to 1814, when Salta was basically concerned with assisting the national armies in the campaigns into Upper Peru. The second phase was the reaction of the salteños to the invasion of Pezuela in 1814, when the province rose against Spanish domination and began the famed gaucho campaigns that hurled back every invading royalist army.

Throughout the first phase of the period the kinship elite supported the military operations of the Army of the North by contributing money and materiel, and by raising companies of soldiers for the Army of the North. The monetary support for the military forces of the Junta of Buenos Aires was greatest in 1810 (see chart, Appendix E). That year the core families and related families contributed over 28,000 pesos to support the army, of which 22,000 pesos came from the Figueroas. After this great monetary contribution, the kinship elite, through its control of the cabildo, shifted the financial burden onto the Spanish merchant community of Salta by a series of forced levies, but it continued to supply basic materials to the army. Notable examples of this type of support were Vicente Toledo's donation of 1,300 horses and Pedro José Saravia's contribution of over 5,000 cattle. This material support was essential to the success of patriot armies and general confidence in the commanders.

The kinship elite was also active in raising and leading companies of volunteers. In 1811 fourteen volunteer companies were raised in the province. Eight of these fourteen were commanded by members of the Figueroa, Saravia, Cornejo, and Toledo families.[66] By 1814 the patriot military disasters in Upper Peru had created doubts about the ability of Buenos Aires to defend the area. By this time the kinship elite had stopped almost all support for Buenos Aires.

In 1814 royalist troops invaded Salta for the second time, and again government forces hastily abandoned the province. Left to their own resources the salteños offered a determined resistance which was led by the kinship elite and its relatives. Success was based on the abilities of the estancieros to lead their own gauchos effectively. Twenty-nine of these individual units are mentioned in treatments of the resistance of 1814, and fifteen of them were led by members of the kinship elite and the associated families.[67] The other fourteen were led by estancieros who may have been connected to the family structure, but whose connection cannot be established from available documents. The principal commanders of these gaucho units were Pedro José Saravia and Martín Güemes, both members of the kinship elite, which by 1814 had assumed complete responsibility for defense.

In considering the monetary contributions to the cause of independence by Salta from 1810 to 1815, the chart in Appendix E should be noted. It covers only voluntary gifts of the kinship elite and the forced levies on the royalist merchants that were collected by the city of Salta.[68] Prior to 1814 these merchants bore the brunt of the tax burden; in 1814, however, the governor, Bernabé Aráoz, opposed a measure passed by the cabildo that would have continued this practice. He was upheld by the government of Buenos Aires, and the names of López, Torino, Aráoz, Arias, Usandivares, Velarde, and Ormaechea began to appear on lists of forced levies.[69] These levies were in January and February, and they probably contributed to hostility towards Buenos Aires, and to the election of Martín Güemes to the governorship in May.

Aside from donations and taxes, the main factor that affected the economic position of the kinship elite was the loss of trade due to the war. While the families comprising its core were not merchants, the family structure included many who were engaged in the sale of mules. Salta's economy always rested on the movement of goods from the Plata to Upper Peru. The war made Salta the end of a trade route rather than its center. When the royalists controlled the city, the route to Upper Peru was opened, but the route to Tucumán was closed. When the patriots were in control the route to Upper Peru was closed. Merchants could only hope for a conclusion to the war that would re-open trails to both Upper Peru and Tucumán.

By 1815 the kinship elite was looking for a leader who would provide stability, military security, a measure of self-government, and who was acceptable to the group. The latter requirement appeared to be met by the return of Martín Güemes. Güemes was a successful military leader, popular with the people, and directly related to the Saravias, Figueroas, and Cornejos, and he had important family connections in Jujuy. Shortly after his return Martín Güemes was elected governor.

NOTES

1. "Letter of Feliciano Antonio Chiclana to the Junta of Buenos Aires, September 1, 1810," in Cornejo, *Historia,* p. 61. See Also "Letter of Feliciano Antonio Chiclana to the Junta of Buenos Aires, December 17, 1810," in Cornejo, *Apuntes,* p. 172.
2. After visiting Salta, I feel that this statement could be even stronger. A recent study of Edberto Oscar Acevedo refers to the structure as an oligarchy wielding complete control. Also in an interview with Atilio Cornejo (March 16, 1967) he concurred completely with the concept of a familial controlled political structure in the province at this time.
3. José María Ots Capdequí, *Manual de historia del derecho español en las Indias y del derecho propiamente indiana.* Buenos Aires, 1945, Chapter III. In the presentation of this thesis regarding the influence of the kinship elite which attaches a great deal of importance to familial ties, the author admits

the acceptance of various theses of other scholars. One, the contemporary Argentine family is patriarchal and is many times stronger than its North American counterpart. (See Arnold Strickton, "Class and Kinship in Argentina," *Contemporary Cultures and Societies of Latin America.* Dwight B. Heath and Richard N. Adams eds.; New York, 1965. pp. 324-342.) Second, Family structures tend to become stronger during periods of national stress or war. (See Carl J. Frederick and Zbigneiv K. Brzezinski, *Totalitarian Dictatorship and Autocracy.* New York, 1961. p. 242.) Three, The Spanish family was stronger in the past than it is at present. (See John P. Gillin, "Some Signposts for Policy," in *Social Change in Latin America Today,* ed. Richard P. Adams. New York, 1960. pp. 33-34.) Four, the family is and was the foremost contributor to the individual's concept of values. (See David Potter, *People of Plenty.* Chicago, 1961. pp. 107, 202-204. Guido de Ruggiero, *The History of European Liberalism,* trans. by R. G. Collingwood, Boston, 1959. p. 230.)

4. Frías, II, 513. See also "Testamento de Dn. Antonio Figueroa, 1790" *Archivo histórico de la provincia.* Escribanía de José Jnto. Tobina, folletos 55-65.
5. Parrish, p. 275.
6. "Letter of Feliciano Antonio Chiclana to the Junta of Buenos Aires, September 1, 1810," in Cornejo, *Historia,* p. 61.
7. "Letter of Feliciano Antonio Chiclana to the Junta of Buenos Aires, December 17, 1810," in Cornejo, *Apuntes,* p. 172.
8. Frías, II, 513.
9. Appendix C.
10. Frías, I, 78.
11. Cornejo, *Historia,* p. 55.
12. Appendix D.
13. *Ibid.*
14. Cornejo, *Apuntes,* pp. 147-148.
15. Appendix C.
16. Cornejo, *Apuntes,* p. 161.
17. "Testamentario de Juan Adrián Cornejo, 1799," *Archivo General de la Provincia,* Rejistro Judical-Carpeta 23 de la Escribanía de don Isidro Matorras, folletos 24-38. Hereafter cited as *AGP.*
18. Cornejo, *Apuntes,* pp. 200-207.
19. "Testamentario de Pedro José Saravia, 1801" *AGP.* Rejistro Judical—Carpeta (no number) del Escribanía de Tarbulino de la Silva, folletos (no numbers). Also "Interview with Dr. Federico Saravia Toledo y Toledo, Salta, March 23, 1967." For more information on the Saravias see Edberto Oscar Acevedo, *La Intendencia de Salta del Tucumán en el Virreinato del Río de la Plata.* Mendoza: Universidad de Cuyo, 1965.
20. Appendix B. See also Frías, II 19 and 99.
21. Appendix D.
22. *Ibid.*
23. "Act of the Cabildo of Salta, May 24, 1821," in Cornejo, *Historia,* pp. 311-312.
24. Cornejo, *Historia,* p. 308.
25. *Ibid.,* p. 78.
26. Appendix C.
27. "Testamentario de Vicente Toledo, 1790" *AGP.* Rejistro Judical-Carpeta (no number) de la Escribanía de José Jnto. Tobino, folletos 70-75. Also

"Interview with Dr. Federico Saravia Toledo y Toledo, Salta, March 23, 1967."
28. Frías, II, 66.
29. Cornejo, *Apuntes,* pp. 736-738.
30. Frías, II, 453.
31. Appendix A.
32. *Ibid.*
33. *Ibid.*
34. *Ibid.*
35. *Ibid.*
36. *Ibid.*
37. *Ibid.*
38. *Ibid.*
39. Frías, II, 528.
40. José Moldes, "Exposición acerca de sus servicios a la causa pública," in Frías, I, 462.
41. This information can be obtained from scattered data in Cornejo, *Historia.*
42. Appendix C. See also Solá.
43. Appendix B.
44. Cornejo, *Apuntes,* p. 636.
45. Appendix A.
46. *Ibid.*
47. *Ibid.*
48. Cornejo, *Apuntes,* p. 622. See also Appendix A.
49. Appendix B.
50. Appendix A.
51. *Ibid.*
52. Appendix B.
53. Appendix A.
54. *Ibid.*
55. *Ibid.*
56. *Ibid.*
57. Appendix B.
58. Appendix A.
59. *Ibid.*
60. *Ibid.*
61. *Ibid.*
62. *Ibid.*
63. Appendix B.
64. Appendix A.
65. *Ibid.*
66. Cornejo, *Historia,* p. 90.
67. Appendix D.
68. For a sample of a forced levy on the Spanish community, see Appendix E.
69. Cornejo, *Historia,* p. 118.

CHAPTER III

The Governorship of Güemes, 1815-1821

Martín Güemes was elected governor of Salta on May 6, 1815. On May 5 the Buenos Aires government had passed the second *Estatuto Provisional* which legalized the election of provincial governors.[1] Since it took at least five days for news to reach Salta from Buenos Aires, it seems likely that the salteños acted before they knew their act would be approved by Buenos Aires.

The Alvear government had fallen without ever receiving the recognition of the salteños, who had sided with Rondeau in his dispute with Alvear. Because of the instability and chaos in Buenos Aires, the salteños simply were not willing to acknowledge any authority beyond their own cabildo. The cabildo therefore named Güemes as governor, and by chance this action was authorized by new national regulations.[2]

The election caused difficulties in the province despite its legality. The other towns of the province—Orán, Tarija, and Jujuy—were not consulted beforehand, but they were asked to approve the action of the cabildo of Salta. The people of Jujuy resented their exclusion from the election, and they were determined to resist Güemes' authority.

On May 15 the cabildo of Salta called for an election of deputies to meet and consider the new government of Buenos Aires. They approved the government of Rondeau and the Estatuto Provisional, and they agreed to the calling of a national assembly to draw up a constitution. The assembly was to meet in a place free of outside pressures. The salteños added a reservation to the effect that, if the assembly had not convened in five months from the date of ratification, sovereignty would revert to the cabildo.[3] Salta thus reassumed her former relations with the national government.

It was not easy to obtain ratification of Güemes' election by the other towns of the province, though Orán and Tarija approved the election immediately. On May 6 news of the election reached Jujuy, and at first the reaction was favorable. On May 8 Güemes sent word that Salta had the right to select the governor in the absence of superior authority, and that Jujuy could select a lieutenant-governor.[4] This had been the custom in the former intendancy, and it relegated Jujuy to an inferior position. Güemes' well-intentioned gesture aroused resentment. Royalists stirred this resentment, until the cabildo of Jujuy protested the election of Güemes and elected one of his enemies as lieutenant-governor. This

24

was Mariano Gordaliza, who withheld recognition of Güemes until a popular assembly could consider his election.[5]

Güemes agreed to mediate the dispute, and the salteño cabildo member, Dr. Arias Velásquez, was appointed as Salta's representative. Dr. Juan Ignacio de Gorriti represented Jujuy. These men met on May 26 and began their arguments. In June the talks were interrupted when Gorriti left to serve with Rondeau's army. The issue remained unresolved.

When Güemes agreed to Jujuy's demand for an assembly to consider his governorship, Orán and Tarija elected deputies. On June 17, however, the cabildo of Jujuy decided to submit the question to Álvarez Thomás, the provisional supreme director. In July word came that the Buenos Aires government had approved Güemes' election. Jujuy postponed settlement of the issue and considered ratification of the Estatuto Provisional.[6] On September 4 the Jujuy cabildo agreed to take part in the assembly, providing it met in a neutral place.[7] The assembly did not take place, for Güemes rode into Jujuy with a military escort on September 12. He announced that his purpose was to mediate the differences between the two cities. On September 18 the cabildo held a secret vote and placed Jujuy under the governorship of Güemes.[8]

In order to strengthen military defenses Güemes created new militia units. Men were organized into units of 20 to 30, under local leaders. These groups were made parts of four divisions under commanders responsible to Güemes. Arms were issued and drills were held. By this method Güemes greatly enlarged the militia that had proved itself effective against Pezuela. The main part of the fighting force was composed of gaucho bands led by their estancieros. By creating the new units Güemes took the first step toward building an army subordinate to himself rather than to individual ranchers.

On his visit to Jujuy Güemes took several hundred rifles from Rondeau's arsenal, for he lacked sufficient weapons for his militia. Rondeau, who was both Supreme Director of the nation and commander of the Army of the North, demanded that the weapons be returned.[9] Güemes submitted Rondeau's order to the cabildo of Salta. The cabildo rejected the demand on the grounds that return of the rifles would cripple Salta's defenses.[10]

In August, 1815, Rondeau issued a manifesto calling Güemes an "anarchist, an enemy of the nation, a tyrant, and the oppressor of freedom."[11] He then turned the matter over to Álvarez Thomás for settlement. The central government reiterated Rondeau's order to return the rifles. Güemes replied that the weapons were vital to Salta's defenses, and that the province had already been occupied by royalist forces on two occasions. He added that the only government that had cause to fear an armed citizenry was one that sought to impose its will by force.[12]

In October the situation became critical, for Güemes learned that a division under Domingo French was marching to reinforce the Army of the North. This crisis produced a rupture among Güemes' supporters. Dr. Arias Velásquez advised him to return the rifles, but Mariano Boedo counseled him to stand firm. Güemes finally submitted the question to the Assembly of Deputies. The decision of the assembly was that the arms were vital to the defense of the province because of the royalist danger and because it was necessary to arm the forts protecting the eastern frontier against attacks by the Indians.[13]

Conflict seemed imminent, but on November 13 French broke the tension by proposing a conference with Güemes. As a result of the meeting French was allowed to move his troops through Salta in groups of not more than fifty men. French complied, and Güemes aided him by supplying his forces with mules, provisions, money, and horses. In addition, two units of the salteño militia were sent along to aid Rondeau.[14]

While these events were occurring Rondeau's army suffered a setback at Viluma on November 29. The army began to retreat, and Güemes attempted to send reinforcements of more than 700 men.[15] While preparations were under way for the departure of this force, word was received of Rondeau's disastrous defeat at Sipe-Sipe.

Instead of sending the reinforcements, Güemes began strengthening the province's defenses, but he sent troops to Jujuy and Tarija to protect Rondeau's retreat. A committee composed of Güemes, Vicente Toledo, and Francisco Aráoz was set up to raise funds. A forced levy on the Spanish merchants was approved, and Güemes and French together organized the defenses of the province.[16] On February 27, 1816, Rondeau commended Güemes for his public spirit.[17]

As soon as Rondeau arrived in Jujuy, in February, 1816, the enemies of Güemes began complaining. They objected to the forced levy on the grounds that it was too high, and they protested the incorporation of all of the gauchos into military units. And finally they reopened the question of the legitimacy of his governorship. On March 15 the cabildo of Jujuy withdrew its recognition of Güemes, and Rondeau marched on Salta.[18] He encountered little resistance, but faced a denuded area. He arrived in Salta on March 20 and, short of supplies, moved south to the Tejada estancia, Los Cerrillos. There he encountered severe gaucho resistance, and since his cavalry had been destroyed by the royalists, he had little to fight with.[19] On March 22, the Figueroas arranged a meeting between Rondeau and Güemes, and an agreement was reached.[20]

Peace was restored between the salteños and Rondeau, and the former agreed to aid in the provisioning of the Army of the North.[21] Rondeau returned to Jujuy, and on April 17, issued a decree stating that his previous charges against Güemes had been unfounded. He acknowledged Güemes as governor, and lauded him for his valor, services, and justice.[22]

With the solution of the internal difficulties, Güemes turned to a more national problem. Tucumán had been selected as the place for the Constitutional Assembly of 1816. In December, 1815, an electoral assembly was set up from the regions of the province; it selected Salta's first representatives: Dr. José Moldes, Mariano Boedo, and Juan Ignacio Gorriti.[23] On July 9, 1816, the Congress of Tucumán issued the Declaration of Independence, which was ratified by the cabildo of Salta later in the month.[24]

Rondeau's army left the province for Tucumán, and Güemes was given command of the vanguard of the patriot forces in the north. At this time Salta was peaceful; the union with central authority was welcome. The royalists had not yet invaded, and the internal disorders had been quieted. Never again in Güemes' lifetime would Salta enjoy such peace.

In 1815 the Wars of Independence were at their lowest point. In 1814 Ferdinand VII had returned to his throne, and Spain began an all-out effort to recover her colonies. Chile was re-occupied; Bolívar was driven out; and Morelos was executed in Mexico. Only the Río de la Plata had not been reconquered. In 1816 the military forces of the Río de la Plata were all that stood between Spain and complete victory. And all that stood between the royalists of Upper Peru and Buenos Aires were the gauchos of Salta. As a secondary result of this increased Spanish activity, new men appeared in important posts. Fernando de Abascal was recalled, and Pezuela replaced him as Viceroy of Peru. Pezuela's position as commander of royalist forces in Peru was filled by General José de la Serna. La Serna was a veteran of the Napoleonic campaigns and brought with him several veteran divisions.[25] By the end of June Güemes was aware of these changes and began anticipating another Spanish thrust into Salta.

In September, 1816, La Serna assumed command of the royalist vanguard at Tupiza, and on December 24 launched his invasion of the Río de la Plata.[26] La Serna's main purpose was to destroy the forces of San Martín in Mendoza, and he had taken lightly the tales of gaucho resistance, which he thought could be overcome by the veteran Spanish cavalry.[27] The early days of the invasion were encouraging to La Serna, and on January 6, 1817, he entered Jujuy after only token resistance en route.

In Jujuy La Serna issued a proclamation to the gauchos, promising no harm to them if they remained in their homes. Reviewing the strength of his army, he promised defeat to anyone who dared to oppose him.[28] Unimpressed by La Serna's threats, in mid-January Güemes ordered his militia and gauchos to attack. La Serna soon found himself confined to the city of Jujuy, cut off from communication with Peru, low on supplies, and subjected to constant attack day and night. When hunger finally forced him to send out foraging parties, they were ambushed and returned with losses and empty-handed.[29]

Dangerously short of supplies and with the morale of his men low, La Serna broke camp and moved on Salta.[30] Every hour of the day and night the Spanish foraging columns were hit from flank or rear. Each attack was damaging. One of the major gaucho successes occurred at the village of Humahuaca, which, protected by trenches and several pieces of artillery, was the fortified post of the rear guard of the royalist army. On February 28 a band of 150 gauchos led by Manuel Eduardo Arias attacked the royalist position. They came from different directions, broke through the royalist defenses, and achieved a complete victory. The gauchos took ninety-five prisoners, as well as artillery, rifles, munitions, two thousand sheep, sixty head of cattle, and sixteen mules. The defeat hurt La Serna badly.[31]

Despite heavy resistance, La Serna arrived at the outskirts of Salta on April 16. Güemes commanded the forces defending the city. The battle lasted until late in the afternoon of April 17. The gauchos hit the royalist cavalry and forced them off the wings of the main force. The royalists regrouped and, supported by La Serna's artillery, began a decisive move on the city. Güemes ordered a retreat, but was disobeyed. The gauchos kept up the pressure until the royalist army entered the city. In the city all was confusion. Friends were shot as enemies, and chaos continued until the royalist forces were able to control the streets.[32]

La Serna immediately re-established order, and during his occupation of the city no excesses were committed. For about a week the city was relatively quiet. Despite Güemes' precautions, La Serna found some provisions.[33] When these were gone, however, the royalists were in a desperate situation.

La Serna knew well the futility of sending out small foraging parties. He organized four strong columns of troops and cavalry to search for provisions. The strongest of these, under the command of Gerónimo Valdés, marched north in the direction of Jujuy. During the night they swung south, and morning found them about thirty miles south of Salta. That afternoon they were discovered, and gauchos flocked into the area. Luis Burla led the attack but soon was joined by bands under Pedro José Zavala, Pablo de Latorre, and Juan Antonio Rojas. During the incessant attacks the royalists were forced to form an infantry square, and in this formation they retreated to Salta.[34] The other columns suffered similar, though not as extreme, damage. The city was encircled by the salteños, and the siege was continued.

On May 6 hunger forced the royalist retreat from Salta, which was harassed all the way to Tupiza. The troops that left Salta were in a critical state, reduced to eating burros and mules. Such was the end of the proud royalist army which had vowed to march to Mendoza.[35]

A curious onlooker, Dámaso de Uriburu, noticed that Güemes did not push his advantage. The advantage was evident in the numerical superiority of the salteño forces. With this in mind, Uriburu felt that an all-out attack would have annihilated the remnants of the demoralized royalist forces.[36] But no such attack was made, and La Serna survived to plague the region in succeeding years.

As soon as the Spanish forces had evacuated the province, complaints were sent to the central government about the counterfeit money coming out of Salta.[37] This was brought to the attention of Güemes, who, in conjunction with the cabildo, redeemed the counterfeit coins at their full value and stopped their further movement.[38] This money, the so-called *plata de Güemes,* was in two-real pieces. When they first appeared they were mostly silver. By the time they were taken out of circulation they were almost pure copper. It should be noted that there was no national law against counterfeiting at the time, but a moral law had been violated.[39] There were many theories regarding the origin of the coins. Vicente López attributed part of the guilt to Güemes, since he allowed the coins to remain in circulation until the central government notified him of its concern in the matter. It seems likely, however, that the coins originated in the mint of Potosí. And since they appeared after La

Serna's invasion, it is probable that they were introduced by the opponents of Güemes.[40] He requisitioned all the false coins and then threatened severe penalties against those who did not turn them in.[41]

Despite these difficulties, military and economic, by 1817 Salta received some good news. In November, on the recommendation of Belgrano, Salta's heroic resistance to La Serna's army was recognized by the national government. A medal was struck and inscribed, "To the merit of Salta—1817."[42] Güemes himself was honored by promotion to the rank of general in the army and a life pension of 400 pesos per year for his oldest son.[43]

In the fall of 1817 La Serna again attempted to penetrate Salta's defenses. He sent a force of 1,000 men under the command of Olañeta south to the valley of Humahuaca. This force was turned back before it reached Jujuy, and in December it retreated to Tupiza. This venture was followed by similar thrusts southward throughout the spring of 1818.[44] The greatest success achieved by these expeditions was a four-day occupation of Jujuy in January.[45] While the presence of the royalist forces did not present a great military threat to the city of Salta, it did force Güemes to keep the province in a state of military preparedness.

The constant military activity in the province presented grave economic problems. By the middle of 1818 Güemes acknowledged that the area was close to economic collapse. In a letter to Pueyrredón he outlined the state of the defenses of Salta. The most serious deficiency was the lack of money to pay the militia. Since the royalists continued to exert pressure from Tupiza, Güemes felt obliged to keep his forces mobilized. Since they had received no pay the gauchos stole what they needed from the estancias.[46] This practice caused complaints from the powerful estancieros, and, since many of them had commands of their own, dissension arose among groups of militia.

Earlier Güemes had attempted to solve the problem of pay for the militia by a primitive agrarian reform law. The act exempted gaucho militiamen from paying rent to the estancieros. This solution failed because the devotion of the gauchos to the estancieros was stronger than their desire for free land, and the gauchos refused to take advantage of the law.[47] This left Güemes with a military payroll that was much higher than the voluntary assistance given by Buenos Aires and Salta. Although he realized that the practice could not last indefinitely, he and the cabildo imposed a forced levy on the royalist community of Salta. By this and similar means they raised over 11,000 pesos for the military.

Most of this money was given to the various commanders for their gauchos.[48]

Despite economic difficulties, relations with the central government remained firm. On April 2, 1818, the cabildo of Salta approved the *Reglamento Provisorio,* and sent it to the cabildo of Jujuy for approval. Among other requirements of the new set of laws, the Reglamento Provisorio called for new elections and the formation of the new Electoral Assembly. Güemes was re-elected governor, and the assembly was elected on May 2, 1818. It met in the spring of 1819 and elected Marcos Salomé Zorilla, Pedro Antonio Velasco, and Guillermo de Ormaechea as deputies.[49]

Early in June Salta received the welcome news of San Martín's victory at Maipú in Chile. This victory prompted optimism among members of the government and the citizenry in general about the end of the war.[50] San Martín's victory had other effects on the province. The royalist pressure on the northern region of Salta temporarily ended as the invading forces pulled back to Tupiza. This respite lasted until the summer of 1819. Maipú also caused Güemes to suspect that Belgrano would launch an invasion of Upper Peru. The campaign did not materialize, however, owing to the chaotic conditions in the rest of the Argentine provinces.

From July, 1818, to the spring of 1819, few records are available for Salta.[51] It seems that the central problem during this period was the prevention of anarchy in the province. Many of the provinces surrounding Salta had refused to acknowledge the authority of Buenos Aires. Within the province itself this created dissident groups who favored provincial independence. Güemes, however, consistently reminded the people that the great enemy of Salta was Spain, and he cautioned them not to let internal division make the area an easy prey for a Spanish army. Finally, in April, 1819, he issued a *bando* at Jujuy. This required all men of the province to register with the government within a period of eight days. They were asked to pledge themselves to obey the laws of the nation and to take up arms to defend the cause of independence. All those who did not wish to take this oath were to be given passports into Spanish territory in Upper Peru.[52] Güemes was congratulated and praised by the press in Buenos Aires for his efforts to hold Salta to the national purpose.[53]

In May of 1819 the cabildo of Salta formally ratified the constitution submitted by the Congress of Buenos Aires. In November senators were elected to represent Salta. The Assembly of Castañanes was composed

31

of representatives of Orán, Salta, and Jujuy. Dr. Manuel Antonio de Castro and Dr. Juan Ignacio Gorriti were elected senators, seconded by Juan Manuel Güemes and Dr. Vicente A. de Echevarría. The representative of the Church was José Ignacio de Gorriti. The representatives to the legislature were still Zorrilla, Velasco, and Ormaechea.[54]

During this period the royalists launched another small offensive against Salta, apparently for the purpose of gathering supplies. The attack began in March of 1819 and continued intermittently throughout the rest of the year. The presence of the royalist threat prompted a voluntary levy upon Salta and Jujuy in March. The total received by this means was 14,400 pesos. In September a forced levy directed against the merchants added 2,668 pesos. In October another forced levy was made on the property of the Spaniards of Jujuy and Salta, which netted 10,900 pesos. These levies did little to cement the province together and created divisions among the followers of Güemes.[55] By 1820 basic problems thus threatened the existence of the Güemes government. Among the most pressing were the localist sentiments manifested in segments of the population, the question of an equitable means of collecting revenue, and the continued threat of invasion. Güemes attempted to solve all three of these problems.

He proceeded with his plans for an all-out invasion of Upper Peru. To finance the project, on April 8 the cabildo of Salta decreed a levy designed to raise 5,000 pesos from the merchants and the general citizenry. The estancieros were asked for 500 horses.[56] Güemes had appealed to the other provincial leaders for aid. The only response was from Pedro José Campos, governor of Mendoza, who pledged 100 horses and 100 mules for the projected invasion.[57] But the invasion plans required continuing financial support. To maintain 900 men in active service Güemes knew that a monthly income of 3,000 pesos was absolutely necessary. He called a special assembly to resolve the problem, and through the president of the assembly presented his project to provide the needed revenues:

1) a 50 per cent tax on the sale of whiskey;
2) a levy of two reales on each load of flour;
3) a government monopoly on the sale of playing cards;
4) a tax of two pesos on each shipment of wine;
5) three pesos on each shipment of coca leaves;
6) five pesos levied on each cart that came into the city or that passed through it en route to Tucumán.
7) two pesos on each barrel of molasses;
8) a fee of 100 pesos on the opening of a business;
9) a 10 per cent tax on all rental income;

10) a 4 per cent tax on all goods sold in the province except wine and whiskey;

11) a fee of four reales monthly on each artisan operating a public shop;

12) a tax of one real on each skin taken in the province.[58]

The plan concentrated the financial burden of the province on the merchants, and it was rejected by the assembly on May 5 in favor of a voluntary donation of from one real to two pesos from every citizen. On May 15 the parts of the Güemes proposal that affected the lower strata of society were approved. These included the tax on skins and hides.[59]

On May 19 these revenue measures were replaced by a plan which divided the 3,000 peso requirement between Salta and Jujuy, 2,000 pesos and 1,000 pesos respectively. Salta's share was to be paid by specific groups within the province.

The breakdown by groups was as follows:

Merchants	440 pesos
Pulperías	117 pesos
Citizens of the city	76 pesos
Estancieros	290 pesos
Church	515 pesos
Public employees	71 pesos
Lawyers	19 pesos
Scribes	8 pesos
Doctors	4 pesos
Others	300 pesos[60]

On May 19 news of a new royalist invasion turned all thoughts to defense. Despite tenacious resistance by Güemes' divisions, the royalists entered Jujuy on May 24 and Salta on May 31. Once again the royalists in Salta found every attempt to leave the city was fiercely resisted by bands of gauchos. On June 8 the royalist army began its retreat to Tupiza.[61]

The royalist army numbered 7,000 men, and it was the largest of the various forces that had come out of Upper Peru.[62] Reports of internal dissension in the northwestern provinces had led the royalists to expect aid from dissident groups.[63] When the expected aid was not forthcoming, Colonel Juan Ramírez y Orozco, the royalist commander, chose retreat rather than another test of strength with the salteños. As it was, he lost about 900 men in the campaign.

As soon as the royalist forces had evacuated the province, Güemes resumed his plans for an invasion of Upper Peru. Not satisfied with the response that Salta had received in her call to other provinces for aid, Güemes proposed to the cabildo of Salta, on July 5, the calling of a provincial congress. More specifically, he outlined a plan for a congress of war to be held at Catamarca. The provinces were to be asked to elect deputies to the congress, which was to be concerned solely with the military aspects of an invasion of Upper Peru.[64] By limiting the subject to military affairs, Güemes hoped to avoid the basic political issues causing the disunion of Argentina. The cabildo accepted the proposal, but it was rejected by the other provincial governments. Juan Bautista Bustos, governor of Córdoba, proposed a more general congress, but Güemes was suspicious of that idea, fearing further disunion.

Despite Güemes' reluctance, in August the Electoral Assembly nominated Juan de la Cruz Monge y Ortega and Juan Ignacio Gorriti as representatives of Salta to the Congress of Córdoba. Juan de la Cruz Monge declined and was replaced by Dr. Manuel Antonio de Castro. Both Gorriti and Castro were instructed to work for the reunification of the nation.[65]

Perhaps Güemes' decision to send representatives to the congress was abetted by his being given the over-all command of the expeditionary army of Upper Peru on July 28, 1820.[66] Again Güemes appealed for aid. Bustos promptly sent Alejandro Heredia and 400 men to Salta.[67] The men arrived with depleted ranks due to large-scale desertions while passing through the province of Tucumán.[68] In September Güemes appointed Francisco Pérez de Uriondo to appeal directly for military assistance from the provincial governments and Buenos Aires. What Pérez received was largely sympathy for the cause. Buenos Aires agreed to supply 4,000 rounds of ammunition and 2,000 pesos, but no troops. The government used the Indian danger as an excuse for its refusal to send men.[69]

By September Güemes had gathered his forces and had organized them to his satisfaction. In November he sent observation parties northward to scout the position of the royalist army, and it appeared that Salta would take part in an offensive for the first time in five years. But this was not to be. Affairs in Tucumán prevented the invasion of Spanish territory.

Since Belgrano had left Tucumán in 1819, conditions favorable to national unity had deteriorated. In September of 1820 the governor of Tucumán, Bernabé Aráoz, former governor of Salta, had proclaimed

Tucumán a free and independent republic. In December Ibarra, governor of Santiago del Estero, broke with Aráoz, and civil war began. Aráoz accepted the challenge, and on February 11, 1821, the forces of Ibarra and Aráoz met at Palmar. The victory went to Santiago del Estero.[70]

Despite the victory Ibarra called on Güemes for support. He claimed that the hostilities with Tucumán prevented Santiago from sending money to support the invasion of Upper Peru.[71] Güemes immediately became interested in the plight of Santiago del Estero. He opened negotiations with Aráoz, but the attempts at mediation resulted in little more than an exchange of charges and countercharges between Güemes and Aráoz. Güemes declared that Aráoz was a tyrant who wished to subject the people of Santiago del Estero to his will.[72] Aráoz countered by saying that Güemes had defected to the royalists.[73]

Aside from the respective governors, the peoples of Salta and Tucumán did not want any conflict. This was particularly apparent in the actions of the cabildo of Tucumán in March of 1821. During that month the cabildo sent three sets of envoys to Güemes trying to avoid warfare.[74] The prospect of war was not popular in Salta either, and the discord produced by the decision to declare war caused the first concrete manifestation of an anti-Güemes party.[75] Despite the wishes of the respective communities, however, arbitration was unsuccessful. The failure of the mediation has been attributed to the fact that the representatives of Tucumán were forced to deal with Alejandro Heredia, commander of Güemes' southern forces. Heredia was one of the few who wanted war, and it is indeed possible that he aggravated hostile feelings.[76] Tucumán ultimately agreed to everything Salta demanded except the removal of Aráoz. This request broke up the negotiations,[77] and a force of salteños under Heredia marched against the city of Tucumán. On April 3 the armies met, and Heredia's men swept into the city, but Aráoz rallied his forces and slowly pushed the salteños back. The net result was victory for Tucumán.[78] It was the largest battle in the struggle, which lasted until June of 1821. At that time a peace treaty was signed between Santiago del Estero and Tucumán. Aráoz was deposed in August, and the republic of Tucumán came to an end.[79]

In the meantime Güemes had left Salta to take personal command of his forces in the north. During his absence the cabildo named José Francisco Gorriti as substitute governor.[80] Gorriti occupied this position until April.

Güemes' planned invasion of Upper Peru was checked in March of 1821 when the royalists launched a counter-invasion. There was heavy fighting in the region north of Jujuy until a royalist force under Guillermo Marquiequi occupied the city. When Gorriti heard of this invasion, he appointed Satúrnino Saravia provisional governor and marched to relieve Jujuy. On April 24, 1821, Gorriti inflicted a serious defeat on the Spanish vanguard, capturing Marquiequi and more than 200 others. The royalists retreated northward to regroup.[81]

Despite this victory, more trouble was in store for the Güemes government. Satúrnino Saravia was a member of an anti-Güemes group called the *Patria Nueva*.[82] This group had shown its strength in the cabildo earlier when Güemes asked for a declaration of war against Aráoz in Tucumán; the vote was eleven to nine for the declaration. In May of 1821, because of the absence of Gorriti and Güemes, this nine-member group controlled the cabildo. Led by Dámaso de Uriburu, the cabildo voted on May 24 to depose Güemes and to replace him with Satúrnino Saravia as governor and José Antonio Cornejo as commander of the militia. The cabildo also resolved to cut short the war with Tucumán, and on May 25 sent a dispatch to Aráoz informing him of the action and appealing for military aid.[83]

The new government was short-lived. On May 31 Güemes re-entered the city at the head of 600 gauchos and reassumed authority. In an attempt to quell the fears of dictatorship, he pledged himself to retire from office as soon as the royalists had been expelled from the province. The members of the rebel cabildo fled, and some took refuge with the royalist army under Olañeta.[84]

When order had been restored, Güemes set up headquarters at Velarde, about three miles south of Salta. Here he began anew to make plans for a move against the enemy. On June 7, 1821, he rode into Salta with an escort of fifty men to visit his sister, Magdalena Güemes de Tejada. As Güemes and his men began to leave that evening, they were challenged and ordered to identify themselves. When they answered that they were patriots, shooting started. Güemes feared another internal revolution, and led his men in an attempt to escape.[85] In reality they faced a royalist force led by a salteño, Luis Archondo, and in the ensuing battle Güemes was critically wounded.[86]

The group finally broke through the royalists, and Güemes was taken to his headquarters at Velarde. Jorge Enrique Widt was given temporary command, and Güemes received the medical assistance of Dr. Antonio Castellanos; even Olañeta offered his personal doctor to the wounded governor. On June 17, 1821, however, Martín Güemes died.[87]

After the skirmish with Güemes, the royalists occupied Salta. Resistance mounted as on previous occasions, despite the absence of Güemes. Led by Gorriti, Cornejo, and Widt, by mid-July the gauchos had starved the royalists to eating dogs.

The death of Güemes permitted the members of the Patria Nueva to recover control of the province. On July 14 the cabildo accepted an armistice whereby the royalists agreed to evacuate the province, and peace was restored. The Patria Nueva held control until September, when the followers of Güemes reassumed control of the province. These events, however, go beyond the scope of this work. Martín Güemes was dead, and his domination of Salta had ended.

NOTES

1. Perhaps this point is unnecessary to the question of legality due to salteño reservations to the Estatuto of 1813. See Sierra, V, 457-458.
2. Cornejo, *Historia*, p. 174.
3. *DHA*, VIII, 52.
4. "Letter of Güemes to the Cabildo of Jujuy, May 8, 1815," in Cornejo, *Historia*, p. 182.
5. *Ibid.*
6. *Ibid.*, p. 181.
7. Frías, III, 372.
8. "Act of the Cabildo of Jujuy, September 18, 1815," in Cornejo, *Historia*, p. 182.
9. *Ibid.*, p. 184.
10. *Ibid.*, p. 188.
11. "Decree of Rondeau, August 11, 1815," in *ibid.*
12. "Letter of Güemes to Álvarez Thomás, October 11, 1815," in *ibid.*, pp. 189-190. See also Frías, III, 440-46.
13. Cornejo, *Historia*, p. 195.
14. *Ibid.*, p. 196.
15. *Ibid.*
16. Frías, III, 460.
17. "Letter of Rondeau to Álvarez Thomás, February 27, 1815," in *ibid.*
18. "Resolution of the Cabildo of Jujuy, March 15, 1816," in *ibid.*
19. *Paz*, p. 337.
20. "Treaty of Los Cerrillos, March 22, 1816," in Frías, III, 514.
21. *Ibid.*
22. "Decree of Rondeau, April 17, 1816," in Cornejo, *Historia*, p. 205. For a general discussion of the difficulties between Rondeau and Güemes and their eventual settlement, see "Letter of Pedro Medrono to a friend in Buenos Aires, March 28, 1816," *DHA*, VII, 161-170.
23. Cornejo, *Historia*, p. 187.
24. *Ibid.*, pp. 218-224.
25. *Paz*, p. 358.
26. Bartolemé Mitre, *Historia de Belgrano y de la Independencia Argentina,* Buenos Aires, N.D., II, 343. Hereafter cited as Mitre, *Historia de Belgrano.*

27. Vicente López, *Historia de la República Argentina*, Buenos Aires, 1913, VI, 448.
28. *Uriburu*, p. 165.
29. Cornejo, *Historia*, p. 233.
30. *Gaceta de Buenos Aires; desde 1810 hasta 1821*, ed. Antonio Zinny, Buenos Aires, 1875, February 22, 1817, p. 118.
31. *Memoria de Gobierno del Virrey Joaquín de la Pezuela*, eds. Vicente Rodríguez Casado and Guillermo Lohmann Villena, Sevilla, 1947, II, p. 136. Hereafter cited as *Pezuela*.
32. *Uriburu*, p. 167.
33. *Ibid.*
34. *Ibid.*, p. 168.
35. *Pezuela*, II, 155. See also Mitre, *Historia de Belgrano*, II, 369-371.
36. *Uriburu*, p. 169.
37. "Letter of Director Pueyrredón to Congress, December 24, 1817," *Documentos del Congreso de Tucumán*: Archivo Histórico de la Provincia de Buenos Aires. La Plata, 1947, XII, 71. Hereafter cited as *DCT*.
38. Cornejo, *Historia*, pp. 246-248.
39. Ricardo, Levene, *Historia de la nación Argentina*, Buenos Aires, 1950, VII, 341.
40. López, VII, 433.
41. "Act of the Cabildo of Salta, December 4, 1817," in Cornejo, *Historia*, p. 248.
42. Mitre, *Historia de Belgrano*, II, 377.
43. *Gaceta de Buenos Aires*, May 31, 1817, p. 237.
44. Cornejo, *Historia*, pp. 249-253.
45. *Pezuela*, II, 242.
46. "Letter of Güemes to Belgrano, April 10, 1818," *DCT*, XII, 105-106.
47. *Uriburu*, p. 142.
48. Cornejo, *Historia*, pp. 254-255.
49. *Ibid.*, pp. 256-258.
50. "Letter of the Cabildo of Salta to San Martín, June 8, 1818," *Documentos para la historia del Libertador San Martín*, Buenos Aires, 1955, VII, 465. Hereafter cited as *DSM*.
51. This is attributed to the loss of records that occurred because of the transfer of the archives in and out of Salta during the Spanish invasions. Miguel Solá, *Erección y abolición del Cabildo de Salta*. Buenos Aires, 1936, p. 20.
52. "Decree of Güemes, April 22, 1819," *Partes oficiales*, III, 85-86.
53. *Gaceta de Buenos Aires*, May 26, 1819, p. 347.
54. Cornejo, *Historia*, p. 267.
55. *Ibid.*, pp. 258-261.
56. "Session of the Cabildo of Salta, April 8, 1820," in Cornejo, *Historia*, p. 272.
57. *Ibid.*
58. "Act of the Electoral Assembly of Salta, May 5, 1820," in *Ibid.*, p. 273.
59. *Ibid.*
60. "Act of the Electoral Assembly of Salta, May 16, 1820," in *Ibid.*, p. 275.
61. "Letter of Güemes to the governor of Córdoba, June 22, 1820," *Partes oficiales*, III, 162-167. See also *Gaceta de Buenos Aires*, June 7, 1820, p. 410.
62. "Letter of Güemes to the governor of Córdoba, June 22, 1820," *Partes oficiales*, III, 162-167.
63. *Pezuela*, II, 721.
64. Cornejo, *Historia*, p. 283.
65. *Ibid.*, p. 269.

66. "Letter of Juan Bautista Bustos to Güemes, June 7, 1820," *Partes oficiales,* III, 318-319.
67. *Ibid.*
68. Cornejo, *Historia,* p. 501.
69. "Letter of the Junta of Representatives of Buenos Aires to Francisco de Uriondo, December 18, 1820," in *ibid.,* pp. 291-292.
70. *Ibid.,* p. 299.
71. *Ibid.*
72. *Ibid.,* p. 301.
73. "Letter of Bernardo O'Higgins to San Martín, June 19, 1821," *Documentos de Archivo de San Martín,* Buenos Aires, 1910, V, 496. Hereafter cited as *DAM.*
74. "Act of the Cabildo of Tucumán March 22, 1821," *Actas del Cabildo: Documentos Tucumanos; 1810-1824,* ed. Manuel Lizondo Borda, Tucumán, 1940, II, 270. Hereafter cited as *DT.*
75. "Act of the Electoral Assembly, February 24, 1821," in Cornejo, *Historia,* p. 303.
76. *Ibid.,* p. 308.
77. "Act of the Cabildo of Tucumán, April 28, 1821," *DT,* II, 270.
78. Col. J. Anthony King, *Twenty-four Years in the Argentine Republic . . . ,* New York, 1846, p. 58.
79. "Act of the Cabildo of Tucumán, August 29, 1821," *DT,* II, 293.
80. Cornejo, *Historia,* p. 309.
81. *Ibid.,* p. 310.
82. *Paz,* p. 452.
83. "Act of the Cabildo of Salta, May 24, 1821," in Cornejo, *Historia,* pp. 311-313.
84. *Paz,* p. 453.
85. "Letter of Colonel Jorge Enrique Widt to Dionisio Puch, April 8, 1866," in Cornejo, *Historia,* p. 318. See also *Paz,* p. 454.
86. *Ibid.*
87. Cornejo, *Historia,* p. 320.

CHAPTER IV

Güemes and the Kinship Elite

The political career of Martín Güemes was outwardly similar to that of other Argentine provincial caudillos. His relations with the kinship elite have been mentioned; now they will be considered in greater detail, for they determined his position and actions from 1815 to 1821.

Güemes' paternal family had little importance in his rise to national prominence. The father was a Spaniard, Gabriel de Güemes Montero, who came to Salta in January of 1778. That year a royal treasury was established in Salta, and Gabriel Güemes was the new treasurer.[1] Perhaps a partial explanation of Gabriel Güemes' ascension from the position of a stranger in the land to one of considerable social status was his marriage on May 31, 1778, to Magdalena de Goyechea y la Corte. The Goyechea family was from Jujuy and dated back to the time of original settlement. Magdalena's mother was, through her maternal line, connected to the Palacios family, which can also be traced back to the settlement of Jujuy.[2] Both of these families, Goyechea and Palacios, were ranking members of the Creole elite of Jujuy, and they had important kinship connections with the elite of Salta.[3] It is probable that the influence of the Goyecheas and Palacios had an effect on the rise of Gabriel Güemes to a position of responsibility.

The marriage of Gabriel de Güemes Montero and Magdalena de Goyechea y la Corte produced nine children. The oldest was Juan Manuel Güemes, followed by Martín, Magdalena, Francisca, Gabriel, José, Benjamín, Isaac, and Napoleón.[4] Of these, only the first six married prior to 1821. All of the marriages were favorable to Martín's rise to power. Juan Manuel Güemes married Bernardina Iriarte, a daughter of a merchant family of Jujuy.[5] Martín Güemes himself married Carmen Puch. Magdalena married Román Tejada, who led the first company of volunteers organized to fight with Balcarce. Francisca married Fructuoso Figueroa de Toledo, and José married Ángela Cerrillo.[6]

Gabriel Güemes Montero died in 1807, and Martín's mother remarried. Her new husband, and consequently Martín's stepfather, was José Francisco de Tineo.[7] Here another link was established between the Güemes family and the kinship elite. The Tineos were an important family, and the daughters of José Francisco, (María and Bárbara) married Vicente Sola and Pedro José Saravia respectively.[8] The Saravia connection was especially important in 1814 when Pedro José Saravia was acting governor of Salta and general military commander of the province. It was at this point that Martín Güemes reappeared in Salta.

Martín Güemes was born in Salta on February 7, 1785. He was baptized Martín Miguel Juan de Mata. His godparents were José González de Prada and María Ignacia Fernández Cornejo y la Corte. The former was Gabriel's superior in his duties in the government, and the godmother was his cousin, the daughter of Juan Adrián Fernández Cornejo and Clara de la Corte y Rosas.[9]

Martín received his first education in a school in Salta and remained in attendance there until he was fourteen. At that age, in 1799, he enlisted in the cadets. While in the cadets he received rudimentary military instruction. In 1805 the company of cadets to which he was attached was transferred to Buenos Aires. It was during this period with the cadets in Salta that he gained an intimate knowledge of the countryside of the area, and of the gauchos.[10]

After his transfer to Buenos Aires Güemes was attached to the staff of Santiago Liniers as an aide. During the English invasions of 1806 and 1807 he participated in the fighting and was promoted to the rank of lieutenant. At this time Güemes heard of his father's failing health and received permission from Liniers to return to Salta. Upon arrival he learned of his father's death and decided to remain there with his family. In 1810 he was incorporated into the garrison of the city ·with the rank of lieutenant.[11]

When the news arrived of the Revolution of May, Güemes enlisted in the ranks of the patriots. He gathered a small group of cavalry and was placed under the command of Diego José de Pueyrredón, who gave Güemes the mission of heading an observation party sent into Upper Peru to scout royalist troop movements and cut off all communications between the royalists in Peru and those in Córdoba. The mission was successful, and soon Güemes was sending Pueyrredón detailed information on royalist activities and strength in the area.[12] As a result of his services in this capacity, Martín Güemes was promoted to captain in September of 1810.[13]

When the army of Balcarce moved into Upper Peru, Güemes was dispatched to raise volunteers in the areas of Tarija and the northwestern sector of the province of Salta. He raised a force of about 800 men, joined Balcarce on November 7, 1810, and took part in the battle of Suipacha that same day. Some historians maintain that his arrival tipped the balance in favor of the patriots; he was, at least, a participant.[14]

41

After the battle of Suipacha Güemes and the leaders of the patriot army fell out. Historians have attributed Güemes' resentment to Balcarce's failure to give him credit for his part in the battle of Suipacha. These accounts, however, all overlook the fact that Güemes' godfather, José González de Prada, was among the first to be executed during Castelli's reign of terror in Upper Peru.[15] This might well have been the most important reason for disenchantment on the part of Güemes. As a result of the rift, Güemes was sent back to Tarija, where he remained until after the defeat at Huaqui.

After the retreat of Balcarce, Juan Martín de Pueyrredón assumed the command of the remnants of the patriot forces. With the change of generals, Güemes' unit was reactivated and began gathering supplies from the countryside. When Belgrano assumed command, Güemes was stationed north of Jujuy in the Quebrada de Humahuaca.[16]

The new commanding officer began hearing unfavorable rumors about the nocturnal behavior of the bachelor officer of the army.[17] As a result of such tales, Güemes was sent to Buenos Aires as escort to a group of prisoners. There he spent the year 1813, totally removed from the province of Salta.

While Güemes was in Buenos Aires, he was attached to the general staff. Later, in November, 1813, he was promoted to lieutenant colonel and took part in the second siege of Montevideo. In December, 1813, news reached Buenos Aires of Belgrano's defeat at Ayohuma, and a military expedition was sent from Buenos Aires to reinforce Belgrano at Tucumán. Güemes was an officer in this force. By the time Güemes arrived he was under a new commander, for José de San Martín replaced Belgrano in January of 1814.[18]

San Martín commissioned Güemes to take command of the defenses of Salta, which he did on March 31, 1814. It must be emphasized, however, that the salteño forces had already been organized and were fiercely resisting the royalist columns that attempted to push south of Salta. The leaders of this resistance were key figures in the kinship elite: Pedro José Saravia, José Antonio Cornejo, Apolinar Saravia, Luis Burla, and other estancieros. The gaucho forces from the estancias were led by their own estancieros. Güemes neither began nor inspired the resistance of Salta; it was already functioning when he arrived. He merely assumed the general leadership of these independent units. His assumption of power was perhaps abetted by the fact that the general command was in the hands of Pedro José Saravia prior to his arrival. Saravia was his step-sister's husband.[19]

The successful defensive campaign against the royalists earned Güemes the respect of San Martín and a great deal of popularity with the people of Salta. After the royalists had been expelled from the area, Güemes was promoted to colonel.

As noted previously, Güemes accompanied Rondeau to Upper Peru, where he and a detachment of salteños participated in the battle of Puerto del Marqués. After this battle he returned to Salta and was subsequently elected governor.

Güemes took over the responsibilities of governor in May of 1815. In July he was married to Carmen Puch. By this marriage he added considerable influence to his family connections, as the Puch family was one of the old families of the province.[20] Three children were born through this marriage; two died in infancy, but the third, Martín Miguel, was governor of Salta in 1847.[21]

The legality of the election of Güemes has been discussed briefly previously. The important issue, why he was chosen, has largely been ignored to this point. Traditional answers to the question do not completely resolve the problem. Most explanations attribute Güemes' election to his military prowess and his tremendous popularity with the masses.[22] Careful scrutiny of these explanations makes them appear questionable.

Güemes' military abilities were impressive, yet after he took command of the salteño resistance in 1814, his participation in combat was negligible.[23] His role in the defense of Salta was as a general commander who was responsible for the co-ordination of combat units and the concentration of all units into a unified military campaign. As a combat commander, Güemes did possess an established reputation, but this was not unique. Other salteños enjoyed equally impressive records.[24] The few raids that he commanded against royalist foraging parties were led in battle by subordinate officers. His greatest contribution to the defeat of Pezuela came from his brilliant organization of vicious defensive warfare.

The second factor traditionally advanced to explain his election, his popularity with the masses, also requires qualification due to the all-inclusive term "masses." This term is often accepted without definition. In Salta "masses" referred to the gauchos, and these included two quite different groups. The first of these was composed of the cowboys who worked on the estancias. Their loyalty was to their *patrón*. The second group was made up of the inhabitants of the southwestern frontier who were known as *coyas*. These coyas corresponded more to the gaucho of literature than did those who worked for the estancieros.[25] The coyas were the greatest personal devotees of Martín Güemes, and they gave him some measure of independent military strength within the confines of the province.

The final objection to the traditional explanation is that Güemes was elected by men who were not members of the masses. They were educated, wealthy, and dominated by the kinship elite. This type of assembly is not apt to act exclusively on the emotional appeal of a candidate. They simply elected a man who was the brother of one member of the cabildo, Juan Manuel Güemes, and who was related to all of the other voting members of the cabildo with the exception of Alberru.[26]

While these family connections certainly made Güemes more acceptable, other factors also worked in his favor. Among these were his status in the national army, the immediate situation of the province, and the fact that Güemes was a predictable figure to the kinship elite. He held the rank of colonel in the national army and was known and respected by nationally prominent figures such as José de San Martín. The reputation and prestige of Güemes became important when the military vulnerability of the province was considered. This factor made a governor known to powerful military leaders of the nation a desirable addition to the provincial government. It should also be added that Güemes had originally been placed in a position of power in Salta by the national government. In this position he had been successful.

Another reason for his election was that the political and military situation of the province required effective leadership. The crisis created by the refusal of the cabildo to recognize the Alvear government left the province without national civil authority. The negation of Alvear was caused by his conflict with General Rondeau. Since Rondeau's forces occupied the province at the time, the cabildo of Salta had little choice but to go along with him. By the spring of 1815, however, Rondeau had left the province and had taken the provincial governor, Hilarión de la Quintana, with him. At this juncture, Güemes re-entered Salta and predicted Rondeau's ultimate defeat. Güemes cautioned the province to begin making defensive preparations to hold back the royalists. These preparations required a capable military organizer, and Martín Güemes was the best qualified of those available.

Perhaps most important to the kinship elite was the predictability and family position of Güemes. His ideas and his qualities, both good and bad, were well known. The elements of the kinship elite were also balanced nicely with Güemes as governor. He was related to each of

44

the families in this elite, yet he was not exclusively a member of any one. Both the Saravia and Figueroa families could approve the choice of Güemes without jealousy. This balance of kinship and Güemes' predictability made him a more acceptable governor than any appointee of Buenos Aires.

Güemes was part of the kinship elite, and the basic question that must be resolved is whether he was able, as provincial caudillo, to amass more power than the group itself. The significance of this type of relationship becomes important when one considers that as long as Güemes represented the group, he reflected its power, and it enjoyed the power of Güemes. Any distinction in regard to Güemes' personal power and that of the kinship elite can only be made on issues about which Güemes and the kinship elite disagreed.

Throughout Güemes' governorship the kinship elite continued to exercise considerable influence in the political, economic, and military affairs of the province. Its members or affiliates constituted an effective majority in the cabildos except for the year 1820.[27] Its influence on taxation was such that the tax rested most heavily on the Spanish merchants or, later, on elements of the society of Salta that were outside the kinship elite. Leading estancieros continued to dominate military affairs, and members of the kinship elite held key positions in Güemes' armed forces.[28]

The cabildo of 1815, which elected Güemes governor of Salta, was dominated by representatives from the family structure.[29] Juan Manuel Güemes, the brother of the new governor, was directly connected to the Figueroa, Cornejo, and Saravia families. Güemes' sister married a Figueroa, his mother's aunt was the wife of Juan Adrián Cornejo, and his stepfather's daughter was the wife of Pedro José Saravia.[30] Miguel F. Aráoz married the daughter of Manuela Figueroa.[31] Alejo Arias was related through family connections to the Saravias, Figueroas, and the Cornejos.[32] Mariano San Millán y Figueroa was primarily connected to the Figueroa family as a consequence of the marriage of María Antonia Figueroa and Francisco G. de San Millán.[33] The relationship of Juan de la Cruz Monge has been established previously, and Inocencio Torino was connected to both the Saravias and Cornejos through marriage.[34] Ángel López was related directly to the Figueroa family by the marriage of Alejandro Figueroa and Benita López.[35] As a result of these family ties, the kinship elite was represented in all but one, Francisco Antonio Alberru, of the members of the cabildo of 1815.

In 1816 the situation was much the same.[36] Gerónimo López, Juan

45

de la Cruz Monge, and Sévero Alvarado were all members of earlier cabildos, and their relationship to the kinship elite has been explained. New members of the cabildo who were related to or part of the structure were Santiago Figueroa, Francisco López, and Facundo de Zuviría. Santiago Figueroa's relation to the kinship elite requires no explanation, and Francisco López shared the general connection of the López family to both the Figueroas and the Cornejos.[37] Facundo de Zuviría was the son of Teresa Castellanos, who, prior to her marriage to Vicente Toledo, had been married to Augustín Zuviría.[38] Again, the cabildo was controlled by those related to the kinship elite.[39]

In 1817 the pattern of domination remained. Members of the family structure who had previously held seats were José D. Fernández, Teodoro López, Francisco López, and Hermenegildo G. de Hoyos. New men connected to the kinship elite were Santiago López, Mauricio San Millán, Pedro A. Ceballos, and Francisco Valdés. Santiago López shared the López family ties to the kinship elite.[40] Mauricio San Millán was directly related to the Figueroa family as a result of the marriage of Francisco G. de San Millán to María Antonia Figueroa.[41] Pedro A. Ceballos was a part of both the Figueroa family and the Cornejo family, due to his marriage to Julián Figueroa, the daughter of Magdalena Cornejo and Francisco Figueroa.[42] Francisco Valdés was related to the Cornejo family through the marriage of Hortensia Valdés to Juan N. Cornejo.[43] Because of these relationships, the kinship elite enjoyed full representation on the cabildo of 1817.[44]

The cabildo of 1818 was made up of six members, four of whom were connected to the kinship elite. The relationships of Juan Manuel Güemes, Ángel López, and Maximiliano López have been discussed, as they held seats on the cabildo prior to 1818. Martín Torino was the fourth member, and he was related to the Cornejo family through the marriage of María Torino to Gabino Cornejo.[45] Again, the kinship elite held the majority of votes on the cabildo.

In 1819 the pattern was identical to that of the preceding year. Out of the six members, four were related to the kinship elite.[46] Maximiliano López and Guillermo de Ormaechea were members of the cabildo before, and were related to the kinship elite through the Güemes family,[47] and Eusebio de Mollinedo was the son of Feliciana Toledo and Lorenzo M. Mollinedo.[48]

In 1820 the pattern of domination of the cabildo was broken.[49] The cabildo was unusually large, thirteen members, and the kinship elite was represented by only four seats. These were held by Pedro Pablo

46

Arias, José D. Fernández, Ángel López, and Juan de la Cruz Monge y Orteaga. All four had held seats prior to 1820.

The next year the kinship elite regained domination of the cabildo.[50] Of the eight members of the cabildo in 1821, five were connected to the dominant families. Two of the five were primary members, Satúrnino Saravia and Baltazar de Usandivares; the other three were members of related families. Satúrnino Saravia's part in the kinship elite is obvious, and Baltazar de Usandivares was the son of Apolinar Usandivares and Manuela Figueroa.[51] Manuel Antonio López shared the López family connections to the structure,[52] and Gaspar José de Solá was directly related to both the Güemes family and the Saravia family.[53] Alejo Arias had held a seat on the cabildo previously, and his relationship has been discussed. The domination of the kinship elite of this cabildo is particularly significant as this was the body that voted to depose Güemes in May of 1821.

Based on the preceding information, it can be stated that the kinship elite dominated the cabildo of Salta during the governorship of Martín Güemes as it had during the period prior to 1815. There was, however, an essential change. After 1815 compliance with national statutes required the election of various types of provincial assemblies that were more or less permanent until a new law, such as the Reglamento Provisorio, required a new election. These assemblies assumed many of the prerogatives that had belonged to the cabildo of Salta. The cabildo became more local in its influence as a result. Thus the composition of the provincial assemblies must be examined before final conclusions about the political power of the kinship elite can be drawn.

Two of these assemblies were called in 1815 to observe separate provisions of the Estatuto Provisionario. The first, the Assembly of Deputies, was a semi-permanent body responsible for provincial legislation. The second, the Electoral Assembly, was a special body called to elect provincial representatives to the Congress of Tucumán.

The Assembly of Deputies was composed of twelve members, eight of whom were associated with the kinship elite.[54] Many of the members of the Assembly of Deputies had held or were later to hold seats on the cabildo of Salta. Among these were Mariano Boedo, Facundo Zuviría, Juan Manuel Güemes, Guillermo Ormaechea, Gerónimo López, and Santiago Figueroa. Their relationship to the kinship elite has been discussed. Others representing the kinship elite were Inocencio Torino, brother of María Torino, who married Gabino Cornejo, and Pablo de Latorre. He was connected to both the Toledo and the Saravia families through the marriage of his sister to José de Ormaechea.[55] These individuals related to the kinship elite were a majority.

The situation was similar in the Electoral Assembly of 1815.[56] Ten members were chosen, and five were members of the kinship elite. Among these were José G. Figueroa, Pablo de Latorre, Gerónimo López, Mariano Boedo, and Francisco Velarde. The family ties of the first four have been mentioned, and Francisco Velarde was connected to the structure through the Güemes family.[57]

In 1820 another Electoral Assembly was called to select representatives to a Constitutional Assembly. It consisted of fifteen members, and the kinship elite can be identified in nine of them. Some had held seats on previously discussed cabildos. Among these were Facundo Zuviría, Pedro Arias Velásquez, Teodoro López, Guillermo de Ormaechea, Gaspar López, Maximiliano López, and José Antonio Cornejo. New to the political scene were Miguel Otero,[58] the son of María Ignacia de Torres, who was a sister of Guillermo Ormaechea's mother, and Juan José Castellanos. He shared the strong Castellanos' connection with the Cornejos and the Figueroas, and married Casilda Saravia.[59] Thus the kinship elite controlled the assembly.

The last Electoral Assembly in this period was called in 1821 to select representatives to a national congress prescribed by the Constitution of 1820. Membership totaled twenty, and the kinship elite was represented by eleven of the members.[60] All of the members representing the kinship elite had held other official positions prior to 1821 or were members of the four basic families. The latter were represented by José Antonio Cornejo, Apolinar Figueroa, Satúrnino Saravia, Pedro Pablo Arias, Juan de la Cruz Monge y Orteaga, Santiago Saravia, and Vicente Toledo. Members related to the kinship elite included Pedro Arias Velásquez, Hermenegildo G. de Hoyos, José D. Fernández, and Santiago López. This assembly was also controlled by the kinship elite, and it was the group that voted on the war against Tucumán.

In short, the political organs of the province of Salta were generally controlled by the kinship elite and associated families. The pattern of political power of this group remained basically the same as it had been in the period from 1810 to 1815. Their power, in the late period, was augmented by the presence of Martín Güemes in the governor's chair as he was also a part of this coterie of wealthy families.

The economic position of the kinship elite during the Güemes administration was similar to that of the preceding four years. While the province was crippled economically by the royalist invasions, the kinship elite's position within the province was relatively unaltered. The four families had their property holdings in the south central region. This region was penetrated briefly by the royalists in 1817, but later invasions of the province were limited to the north until 1821. The economic position of the kinship elite, while considerably less in value of property, thus remained relatively strong.

The military power of the families associated with the kinship elite decreased somewhat during the period from 1815 to 1821. The estancieros still held the commands of the majority of gaucho units, but Güemes increased his military power. This was accomplished by his regularization of the militia of Salta. The province was divided into military districts, each with its own commander. Güemes also set up new units of militia under more professional officers. Examples of these were the vanguard to the north under the command of Rojas, and the command of Jorge Enrique Widt, a veteran of the Napoleonic campaigns, of the resistance of 1821. Güemes revealed his desire to professionalize salteño military forces through extensive drilling, parades, and in his attempts to find professional officers to lead the gaucho units.[61] The growth of Güemes' military power was unimportant as long as his policies and those of the kinship elite were compatible and members of the kinship elite held key positions in his military organization.[62]

On most issues throughout the Güemes regime the kinship elite was in accord with the actions of the governor. It supported Güemes in the negotiations with Jujuy in 1815, in his refusal to surrender the rifles to Rondeau, in his efforts to unify the province, and his actions that stopped the counterfeiting of money. The only examples of discord between it and Güemes were his land reform ambitions, his proposal to change the tax system, and the war with Tucumán.

The land reform was proposed by Güemes in a time of war, so the cabildo of Salta was not consulted. The gauchos did not take advantage of the action and stood firmly with their various estancieros. The old system continued without change.[63] Perhaps Güemes' motive in this proposal was to undermine the military power of the estancieros. As long as the gauchos gave their first loyalty to their patróns, Güemes was not in complete control of his army. This division of loyalty was undoubtedly repugnant to a professional soldier of Güemes' caliber.

The tax reform program was formulated to provide a regular income to support Güemes' offensive military objectives. The proposal was voted

49

down by the Electoral Assembly, and a compromise program was accepted. It should be noted that the compromise which was accepted placed the burden of taxation on groups essentially unrelated to the kinship elite. These were the Church, small businessmen, and the urban citizenry.

The war with Tucumán was much more serious than anticipated, and a conflict over it arose between Güemes and the kinship elite. Güemes' motives for attacking Tucumán have been discussed elsewhere. The kinship elite and the associated families were opposed to the war, for it would close Salta to trade with Tucumán. The issue finally came to a vote in the Electoral Assembly of 1821, and the vote was eleven to nine in favor of the war.[64] The votes revealed that the kinship elite were divided in their opinions. For instance, Santiago Saravia voted against the war, and Satúrnino Saravia voted for Güemes' proposal. Soon events outside the control of either the kinship elite or Güemes changed the situation.

In March of 1821 the royalists began activities in the north. In April the salteño army that was sent against Tucumán was completely defeated. As a result, by May of 1821 Salta faced threats from both the north and the south. Güemes left Salta to take command of the vanguard in the north and appointed José Francisco Gorriti to act as governor in his absence.[65] Soon the royalists were threatening Jujuy, and Gorriti left Salta to give military support to the units defending the neighboring city. This left the cabildo in the hands of the kinship elite. On May 24, 1821, the cabildo voted to remove Güemes from office, and denounced him as a tyrant and a dictator, as was the fashion of the time. The cabildo's next step was to make peace with Tucumán, for this was the reason for removing Güemes. Satúrnino Saravia was appointed interim governor, and José Antonio Cornejo, who was not present, was appointed military commander of the forces of the province.[66]

This action against Güemes by the cabildo has been described by historians as the work of an anti-Güemes party, the Patria Nueva, against the followers of Güemes, the Patria Vieja.[67] It should be emphasized that the Patria Nueva was composed of members of the kinship elite[68] who had supported Güemes since 1815, and that the Patria Vieja was represented by Güemes and José Francisco Gorriti and some supporters in Jujuy.[69] This action of the cabildo was thus the first real rupture between Güemes and the kinship elite.

This break between Güemes and the kinship elite provided the only real test of power. But before the issue could be resolved, it was cut short by an "accident," the timely death of Güemes.

After his removal, a reunion of interests was effected. The war with Tucumán came to an end, and the forces of the kinship elite under José Antonio Cornejo, Apolinar Saravia, and Luis Burla, joined with the forces of Güemes and forced the royalists out of Salta.[70] On July 14 an armistice was signed, by which the royalists agreed to evacuate the province. The cabildo that negotiated and approved this armistice was dominated by the kinship elite, and was headed by Satúrnino Saravia and José Antonio Cornejo.[71] The same family structure thus controlled the destiny of Salta in 1821 as in 1810, the period covered by this work.

The test of power between Güemes and the kinship elite was resolved by his death. Some of the circumstances surrounding this incident would indicate that the royalists were aided in their mission. The first curious incongruity was that a royalist force of such size could enter Salta without being observed. This bears a marked contrast to previous descriptions of gaucho surveillance of royalist movements.[72] The second curious feature was the reaction of Güemes when he discovered the trap. He immediately assumed that it was an internal movement.[73] Finally, it must be noted that there is some evidence that the royalists were guided into Salta by some gaucho leaders such as Pedro Zavala and Ángel M. Zerda.[74] Certainly Güemes was killed by royalist soldiers, but it is suggested that his death was not necessarily the result of a chance encounter, and the fortuitous end of the power struggle between Güemes and the kinship elite may have been no "accident."

In summing up the relationship of the kinship elite to Martín Güemes, the continued influence of the family structure was evident. On points of discord between Güemes and the kinship elite, the family structure was always the victor. Güemes appeared to have been successful only as long as his program was amenable to the families that controlled the province. It is clear, therefore, that the role of Martín Güemes from 1815 to 1821 was that of the representative of a group rather than its ruler.

Martín Güemes was only one of many provincial caudillos who arose in the Plata region during and after the Wars of Independence. The situation of Salta was somewhat different from that of other provinces because of its isolation and strategic location. Except for the Banda Oriental, where a royalist garrison held out for a few years after 1810 and where Portuguese Brazil posed a serious threat, the Plata provinces were never in danger of reconquest. The royalists of Upper Peru were a constant threat to Salta, and their invasions forced on the salteños a measure of cooperation and unity not present elsewhere.

Had the external threat not been present, it seems likely that the major families would have selected a civilian rather than an army officer as governor. This civilian probably would have qualified as a provincial caudillo, and the source and extent of his power would have been similar to those of Güemes.

This study has demonstrated that in Salta the caudillo was merely the agent of the dominant group, the kinship elite. Despite his acknowledged popularity with certain gaucho elements, he had no personal power that would enable him to go against the wishes of his patrons. In each test of power with the kinship elite he lost, and in the last instance he was killed by a royalist patrol under circumstances which can only be noted as mysterious.

The value of this case study is in the approach to the phenomenon of caudillismo in Latin America. There has been much speculation about the sources of caudillo power but no clear and meaningful analysis. This failure may be because the problem has been approached with too great a degree of Anglo-Saxon orientation, as if it concerned state and local government.

It is not suggested that what has been said of the kinship elite and power structure of Salta is applicable to Latin American caudillos in other regions and other eras. It appears, however, that a similar approach to the question of power might be more fruitful than the interpretations thus far employed. Only when similar case studies have been made will it be possible to know if the present study has wider validity.

NOTES

1. Cornejo, *Historia*, p. 48.
2. *Ibid.*, p. 24.
3. Appendix A.
4. *Ibid.*
5. Teófilo Sánchez de Bustamante, *Biografías históricos de Jujuy,* Tucumán, 1957, p. 100.
6. Appendix A.
7. Cornejo, *Historia*, p. 29.
8. *Ibid.*
9. *Ibid.*, p. 46.
10. *Ibid.*, pp. 48-50.
11. *Ibid.*, pp. 52-53.

12. "Letter of Feliciano Antonio Chiclana to the Junta of Buenos Aires, October 20, 1810," in Cornejo, *Historia*, pp. 71-72.
13. "Letter of Feliciano Antonio Chiclana to the Junta of Buenos Aires, September 18, 1810," in *ibid.*, pp. 78-84.
14. For a full discussion of Güemes' role in the battle of Suipacha, see *ibid.*
15. "Report of Castelli to the Junta of Buenos Aires, November 9, 1810," in *Partes Oficiales*, I, 48.
16. Cornejo, *Historia*, p. 91.
17. *Ibid.*, p. 96.
18. *Ibid*, p. 99.
19. Appendix A.
20. *Ibid.*
21. Cornejo, *Apuntes*, p. 504.
22. For the traditional explanation of this event, see Cornejo, *Historia; Paz;* Mitre, *Historia de Belgrano;* and Frías.
23. Bartolomé Mitre, *Estudios históricos sobre la revolución argentina: Belgrano y Güemes,* Buenos Aires, 1864, p. 106.
24. *Ibid.*, p. 104.
25. See Chapter I.
26. Appendix B.
27. *Ibid.* The exception of 1820 can be explained by the fact that the provincial assembly of that year was dominated by the family group.
28. Appendix D.
29. Appendix B.
30. Appendix A.
31. *Ibid.*
32. *Ibid.*
33. *Ibid.*
34. *Ibid.*
35. *Ibid.*
36. Appendix B.
37. Appendix A.
38. *Ibid.*
39. Appendix B.
40. Appendix A.
41. *Ibid.*
42. *Ibid.*
43. *Ibid.*
44. Appendix B.
45. Appendix A.
46. Appendix B.
47. Appendix A.
48. *Ibid.*
49. Appendix B.
50. *Ibid.*
51. Appendix A.
52. *Ibid.*
53. *Ibid.*
54. Appendix B.
55. Appendix A.
56. Appendix B.

57. Appendix A.
58. Cornejo, *Apuntes,* p. 516.
59. Appendix A.
60. Appendix B.
51. King, p. 62.
62. Appendix D.
63. Uriburu, p. 142.
64. Appendix B.
65. See Chapter III.
66. "Act of the Cabildo of Salta, May 24, 1821," in Cornejo, *Historia,* pp. 311-313.
67. For example, see *ibid.,* pp. 314-316.
68. Appendix B.
69. There seems to have been a coterie of families in Jujuy that were connected to the kinship elite of Salta. This connection was weakened by the *jujeños'* devotion to the status of Jujuy. The group was headed by the Gorritis, Goyecheas, and Bustamentes, and supported the brief Gorriti government in 1822.
70. Cornejo, *Historia,* p. 327.
71. *Ibid.,* p. 332.
72. An example of this was the siege of Salta in 1817.
73. "Letter of Colonel Jorge Enrique Widt to Dionisio Puch, April 8, 1866," in Cornejo, *Historia,* p. 318.
74. *Ibid.,* p. 320.

APPENDIX A

THE KINSHIP ELITE

Guide to Appendix A:

FIRST GENERATION IN CAPITALS

Second generation in italics

Third generation simply listed under appropriate parents

THE FIGUEROA FAMILY[1]

ANTONIO DE FIGUEROA—MARÍA DE TOLEDO PIMENTAL

Gabriel[2]
Francisco J.—Magdalena Cornejo
Juana E.—José F. Castellanos
Juliana—Pedro A. Ceballos
Petrona—Juan F. Cornejo
Francisco—Grimanesa Arias
Pedro J.—Lina Figueroa
Josefa F.—Policarpo Matorras
Juan—Josefa Heredia
Miguel A.—Gregoria San Millán
Ventura—Celedonio Fernández

Manuela—Apolinar Usandivares
María J.—José Antonio Cornejo
Rafael—Angela San Millán
María I.—Miguel Aráoz
Baltazar—Mercedes Arenales

Trinidad—Pedro Aráoz
Euligio—?
Mercedes—Mariano Figueroa Aráoz
Francisco—?

Vicenta—Pedro J. Ibazeta[3]

Fructuoso—Francisca Güemes
Mercedes—Miguel Murúa
Miguel—Delfina Ovejero
Eustoquio—Manuela Otazo
José—Damasena Goyechea
Catalina—Francisco Costas

Narciso—Gabriela Goyechea
Alejandro—Benita López
Clara—N. Goyechea
Eugenio—Cornelia Cornejo
Damasena—José Figueroa Güemes
Melchora—Gregorio Cornejo

Santiago—Isabel Aráoz
Pío—Genoveva Paz
Mariano—Mercedes Aráoz Figueroa

Apolinar—María M. Cornejo
Isabel—José L. López
Pedro—?
Dionisia—Maximiliano López
Dámaso—?
Lina—Pedro J. Figueroa

María Antonia—Francisco G. de San Millán
Manuela—Juan de la Cruz Monge y Orteaga

[1]This information was found in Cornejo, *Apuntes* . . . pp. 738-39.
[2]Gabriel was a priest and had no children.
[3]No information was available on the family of Vicenta and Pedro J. Ibazeta.

THE CORNEJO FAMILY

ANTONIO F. CORNEJO—MARÍA CASTELLANOS[1]

Gabino—María C. Torino
María—A. Pardo

Magdalena—Francisco J. Figueroa
Luciana—Juan Pablo Arias

55

MARTÍN GÜEMES

JUAN ADRIÁN FERNÁNDEZ CORNEJO—CLARA DE LA CORTE Y ROSAS[3]
Juan José—Micaela F. Cornejo
  Manuela—Felipe Herédia
  Juana—Alejandro Herédia
  Faustina—Braudio Cornejo y Cornejo
María Ignacia—Lorenzo Goyechea
  Gabriela—Narciso Figueroa
María Mercedes—Apolinario de Figueroa[4]
José Antonio—Gertrudis de Medeiros
  Gregorio Antonio—Melchora Figueroa
José Antonio—María Josefa de Usandivares[2] (second marriage)
  Telésforo—Momenta Castellanos
  Cornelia—Eugenio Figueroa
  Mariano—Presentación Latorre
  María—Juan José Saravia
  Juan Nepomuceno—Azucena Aráoz; and Hortensia Valdés
  Adrián—Avelina Lazcano
  Domingo—?
  Francisco—Juana López

PEDRO VICENTE CORNEJO—ROSA CEBALLOS
Tiburico—Ventura Boeda[5]

[1]Antonio, Juan Adrián Fernández and Pedro Vicente Cornejo were brothers.
Cornejo, *Apuntes* . . . p. 15. For information on the family of Antonio F. Cornejo
see Cornejo, *Apuntes* . . . pp. 145-149.
[2]*Ibid.*, p. 148.
[3]See *Ibid.*, p. 168.
[4]For this family see p. 82.
[5]See Cornejo, *Apuntes* . . . p. 15.

THE SARAVIA FAMILY[1]
JOSÉ SARAVIA—DA. JOSEFA AGUIRRE PERFÁN DE RIVERA

José—Martina Jáuregui
Martín—Petrona Gallo
Pedro P.
Mateo—?
Mariano—Teodora Maurin
Santiago—Josefa Tejada
José M.—Benita Zambrano
Satúrnino—Luisa Saravia and
  Benita Toreno
Antonia—Pedro Pablo Arias
Pedro P.—Manuela Arias
  Castellanos
Pedro A.—María Josefa Corte
María—Lucas Zambrano
Laureana
Monica
Francisca

Casilda—Juan Castellanos
Manuel
Josefa
José
Eusebio

María F.—Valeriano Arias
Santiago
Dominga
María

Juana—Juan B. Castellanos
Juana—G. Castellanos
Marcos—?
Gaspar—?
Josefa—?
Remigo—?
Antonio—Dominga Plazaola

56

JOSÉ SARAVIA (Second Marriage)—JOSEFA ARIAS

Alejandro

Ignacio—*Manuela Fernández*
Nicólas—?
Manuel—?
Aniceta—?

Isabela—*José Burla*

Nieves—*Juan D. Toreno*

María

Pedro José—*Bárbara Tineo*
Apolinar—J. Plazaola
Wences—Pío Saravia
José D.—Josefa López
Eduvigis—Valetín Falcón
Juana M.—?
Asunción—Victoriano Solá
María J.—Camilio Pardo
Milagros—?
Rudecinda—Guillermo
    Ormaechea
Leona—?

[1]This information was found in Cornejo, *Apuntes* . . . pp. 508-509.

THE TOLEDO FAMILY[1]

FRANCISCO DE TOLEDO PIMENTAL— JUANA CRISOSTOMA HIDALGO Y MONTEMAYOR

María[2]—*Antonio de Figueroa*

Pastora—*Juan Francisco de Alvarado*[4]

Vicente—*Feliciana Castellanos*[6]

Bonifácio—*Inés de Burla*[3]

Feliciana—*Lorenzo M. Mollinedo*[5]

[1]This information was found in Cornejo, *Apuntes* . . . pp. 736-38.
[2]María was the mother of the whole chain shown in "The Figueroa Family," p. 143.
[3]Inés de Burla was the sister of Luis Burla, one of the most successful gaucho leaders. He married Teresa Gaona, the daughter of Calixto Gaona, a key member of the cabildo in 1810.
[4]Juan Francisco de Alvarado was a brother of Sévero and Ángel Alvarado, who held seats on the cabildo.
[5]Lorenzo Mollinedo and Feliciana Toledo were the parents of Eusebio Mollinedo, a close associate of Güemes and member of the cabildo in 1819. He married Concepción de Ormaechea, the sister of Guillermo de Ormaechea who was a member of the cabildo several times. Guillermo, in turn, married Rudecinda Saravia, thus establishing another important kinship connection.
[6]Feliciana Castellanos was married before to Agustín Zuviría.

THE FAMILY CONNECTIONS OF GÜEMES[1]

THE MATERNAL FAMILY OF GÜEMES

Martín Miguel de Goyechea—Ignacia de la Corte y Rosas[2]

Lorenzo—María I. Cornejo
Gabriela—Narciso Figueroa y Toledo
Esteban

María Magdalena—Gabriel de
    Güemes Montero
    and
    José Francisco de Tineo[3]

THE GÜEMES FAMILY

Gabriel de Güemes Montero—María Magdalena de Goyechea

Juan Manuel—Bernardina Iriarte   Martín—Carmen Puch
Magdalena—Román Tejada   Francisca—Fructuoso Figueroa
Gabriel   y Toledo
José—A. Cerrillo   Benjamín
Isaac   Napoleón

THE PUCH FAMILY

Domingo Puch—Dorotea Velarde

Juan de la Cruz—María M. Arias   Manuel—Juana M. Gorriti
Carmen—Martín Güemes   Gerónimo
Dionisio

[1]This information was obtained from scattered data in Cornejo, *Historia* . . .
[2]Ignacia de la Corte y Rosas was the sister of Clara de la Corte, who was the wife of Juan Adrián Fernández Cornejo.
[3]José Francisco Tineo had two daughters by a previous marriage, María Felipe and Bárbara. María Felipe married Vicente Solá, and Bárbara married Pedro José Saravia. This information was obtained from an interview with Dr. Federico Saravia Toledo y Toledo. Salta, March 23, 1967.

THE CONNECTION OF THE GÜEMES FAMILY TO THE ARISTOCRATIC ELITE OF SALTA[1]

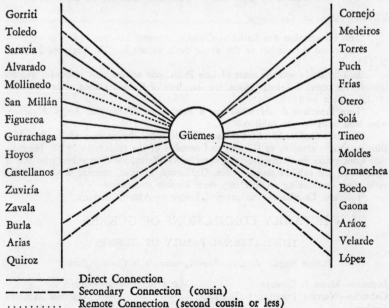

Left	Right
Gorriti	Cornejo
Toledo	Medeiros
Saravia	Torres
Alvarado	Puch
Mollinedo	Frías
San Millán	Otero
Figueroa	Solá
Gurrachaga	Tineo
Hoyos	Moldes
Castellanos	Ormaechea
Zuviría	Boedo
Zavala	Gaona
Burla	Aráoz
Arias	Velarde
Quiroz	López

——————— Direct Connection
— — — — — Secondary Connection (cousin)
. . . . Remote Connection (second cousin or less)

[1]This list was obtained from Frías, I, 78.

SAMPLE CONNECTIONS OF OTHER FAMILIES
TO THE FAMILY STRUCTURE[1]

Brothers GÜEMES———Vicente Solá—
Teodoro López— María F. Tineo
Manuela Frías   their son Manuel
   married
Santiago López— Josefa Chavaria y Moldes
Trinidad Frías   the daughter of
   Manuela Antonia Moldes
Gerónimo López—   the sister of
Juana Moro José Moldes

Maximiliano López————FIGUEROA
Dionisia Figueroa

   Pablo de Latorre
   the brother of
Pedro Arias Velásquez————SARAVIA María A. de Latorre
Antonia Saravia   the wife of
   their son José de Ormaechea
Dr. Pedro A. Arias   the father of
   Velásquez TOLEDO———Concepción—Eusebio Mollinedo
   and
SARAVIA———Guillermo—Rudecinda Saravia

Hermenegildo A. de Hoyos
   the son of
José Domingo de Hoyos
   and
Francisca Aguirre
   the sister of
Josefa Aguirre————SARAVIA

[1]Other connections of this variety can be found in Cornejo, *Apuntes* . . . pp. 495-501, 576-581, 680-738.

FAMILIES DIRECTLY CONNECTED WITH THE
FIGUEROAS AND THE CORNEJOS AND
THE NUMBER OF CONNECTIONS

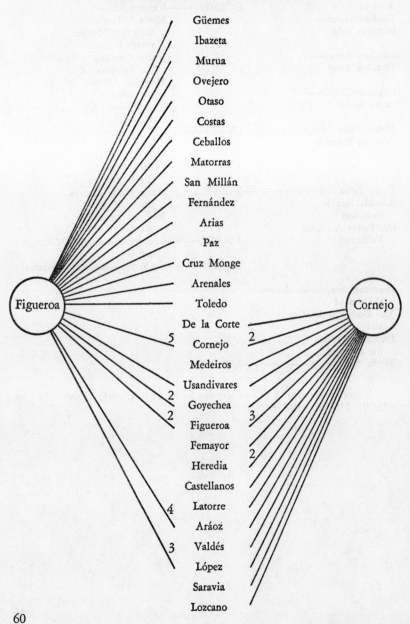

APPENDIX B

THE POLITICAL POWER OF THE KINSHIP ELITE

KEY TO THE CODE USED IN THIS APPENDIX

Cornejo—C, c
Figueroa—F, f
Toledo—T, t
Saravia—S, s
Güemes—G, g

A capital letter indicates a connection more intimate than that of a cousin, which includes brothers, uncles, sons, brothers-in-law, and their female counterparts.

A lower case letter indicates a connection of either first or second cousin. Note:

The information in this appendix was obtained from scattered data in Cornejo, *Historia . . .*

PERCENTAGE OF REPRESENTATION—1810-1821

Cabildos[1]		*Special Assemblies*[2]
36	C	25
28	c	14
52	F	32
10	f	14
17	S	18
30	s	18
17	T	18
40	t	21
19	G	10
30	g	22

[1]Seventy per cent of the cabildo members from 1810 to 1821 were directly connected to the kinship elite.

[2]Fifty-eight per cent of the members of Special Assemblies were directly related to the kinship elite.

COMPOSITION OF THE CABILDO OF SALTA
1810-1821

1810—Governors: Nicolás Severo de Isamendi and Feliciano Antonio Chiclana
Mateo Gómez Zorrilla
José Antonio Fernández Cornejo .... CFSGt
Calixto Ruiz Gaona .... st
Nicolás Arias Rengel .... FCSt
José Francisco Boedo .... Cf
Juan Antonio Murúa .... Fct
Juan Esteban Tamayo

61

1811—Governors: Tomás de Allende and Pedro José Saravia
    Dr. Pedro Arias Velásquez .... SFg
    Francisco Aráoz .... FCt
    Juan Antonio Moldes .... gs
    Juan José Fernández Cornejo .... CFSGt
    Pedro José Saravia .... SGCt
    (Provisional Junta replaced the cabildo in 1811 and 1812)

1812—Governors: Pedro José Saravia and Manuel Belgrano
    (Provisional Junta)
    Pedro José Saravia .... SGCt
    Dr. Pedro Arias Velásquez .... SFg
    (Cabildo re-established under Belgrano)
    Álvarez de Arenales .... Fct
    Gerónimo López .... FCts
    Calixto Sansefenea
    Juan M. Quiroz
    Fructuoso Figueroa .... FGCTs
    Mateo Jimeno
    A. Alvarado .... TFcg
    Isidoro de Matorras .... FCtgs

1813—Governors: Belgrano, Hermenegildo G. de Hoyos, and Chiclana
    Hermenegildo G. de Hoyos................................... s
    Mariano Boedo .... Cfgt
    Guillermo de Ormaechea ....STcfg
    José D. Fernández .... FCtgs
    Teodoro López .... FCts
    Severo Alvarado .... TFcg

1814—Governors: Chiclana, Bernabé Aráoz, and Hilarión de la Quintana
    Gerónimo López ....FCts
    Gaspar Arias ....Fcs
    Guillermo de Ormaechea .... STcfg
    Juan M. Quiroz
    Juan de la Cruz Monge y Orteaga .... FCTGs
    Agustín José de Arteago
    José de Gurrachaga

1815—Governors: Quintana and Martín Güemes
    Miguel Francisco Aráoz ....FCGTs
    Alejo Arias ....Fcgt
    Mariano San Millán y Figueroa............................Fcgt
    Juan de la Cruz Monge y Orteaga .... FCTGs
    Juan Manuel Güemes ....GFCts
    Inocencio Torino ....Sc
    Francisco Antonio Alberru
    Ángel López ....Fcgt

1816—Governor: Martín Güemes
    Juan M. Quiroz
    Santiago Figueroa .... FCTGs
    Gerónimo López .... FCts

Francisco López .... FCts
Juan de la Cruz Monge y Orteaga .... FCTGs
Facundo de Zuviría .... TF
Severo de Alvarado ....TFcg
José A. Zavala

1817—Governor: Martín Güemes
Teodoro López .... FCts
Santiago López .... FCts
Francisco López .... FCts
Mauricio San Millán .... Fcgt
Pedro A. de Ceballos... FGct
Francisco Valdés .... Cfgs
Hermenegildo G. de Hoyos................................... s
José D. Fernández .... FCtgs

1818—Governor: Martín Güemes
Juan Manuel Güemes .... GFCts
José de Gurrachaga
Ángel López .... Fcgt
Maximiliano López .... FCTGs
Martín Torino .... CFgs
León J. Urteaga

1819—Governor: Martín Güemes
Gerónimo Puch .... Gfc
Guillermo de Ormaechea .... STcfg
Maximiliano López .... FCTGs
Eusebio de Mollinedo .... TFcg
José Toribio Tedir
Francisco Claudio Castro

1820—Governor: Martín Güemes
Pedro Pablo Arias .... FScgt
José Joaquín Díaz de Bedoya
Juan Francisco Zamudio
Bonifacio José Huergo
José D. Fernández ....FCtgs
Ángel López .... Fcgt
Dr. Pedro Buitrago
Dr. José Inocencio de Astigueta
Francisco Guzmán
José Alexo de Yanzi
Juan M. Quiroz
Juan de la Cruz Monge y Orteaga......................... FCTGs
Francisco de Uriondo

1821—Governors: Martín Güemes and Satúrnino Saravia
Satúrnino Saravia .... SCftg
Manuel Antonio López .... Fcgt
Baltazar de Usandivares ....FCgts
Gaspar José de Solá .... GSftc

63

Dámaso de Uriburu
Mariano Antonio de Echazu
Alejo Arias .... Fcgt
Francisco Fernández Maldonado .... Fcgt

SPECIAL ASSEMBLIES OF THE PROVINCE OF SALTA

November, 1815—Assembly of Deputies
Dr. José Redhead
Dr. Mariano Boedo .... Cfgt
Dr. Facundo Zuviría .... TF
Dr. Manuel Ulloa
Dr. Juan Manuel Güemes .... GFCts
Guillermo de Ormaechea .... STcgf
Gerónimo López .... FCts
Pablo de Latorre .... TS
Santiago Figueroa .... FCTGs
Juan M. Quiroz
Inocencio Torino .... Sc
Mariano Cabezón

December, 1815—Electoral Assembly
Dr. José Redhead
José A. Zavala
José Gabriel Figueroa .... FCTGs
Francisco Guzmán
Félix Delgado
Pablo de Latorre .... TS
Gerónimo López .... FCts
Dr. Mariano Boedo .... Cfgt
Francisco Velarde .... Gcf
Juan M. Quiroz

May, 1820—Electoral Assembly
Dr. Facundo Zuviría .... TF
Dr. Pedro Arias Velásquez .... SFg
Teodoro López .... FCts
Juan M. Quiroz
Guillermo de Ormaechea .... STcgf
Toribio Tedin
Gaspar López .... FCts
Maximiliano López .... FCTGs
Bartolomé Méndez
José Mariano Bárcena
José T. Otero .... ts
Manuel Francisco Basterra
Manuel de T. Pinto
Juan José Castellanos .... CFTSg
José Antonio Cornejo .... CFTGS

February, 1821—Electoral Assembly
    Dr. Francisco Claudio Castro
    José Antonio Cornejo .... CFTGS
    Manuel Lanfranco
    Apolinar Figueroa .... FCTGs
    Satúrnino Saravia .... SCftg
    Juan M. Quiroz
    Dámaso Uriburu*
    Pedro Pablo Arias* .... SFcgt
    José Lorenzo Olmos
    Mariano Zabala
    Dr. Pedro Arias Velásquez* .... SFg
    Dr. Juan de la Cruz Monge y Orteaga .... FCTGs
    Santiago Saravia* .... SCfg
    Juan Carrillo Albornez
    Vicente Toledo .... TFcg
    Mariano José Ulloa*
    José M. Fernández* .... FGct
    Santiago López* .... FCts
    José M. Arze*

*This identifies those who voted against the war with Tucumán in 1821.

APPENDIX C

THE COLONIAL POSITION OF THE KINSHIP ELITE

ESTABLISHMENT OF A ROYAL TREASURY

In 1778 a Royal Treasury was established in Salta with the assistance of the leading citizens, who pledged 500 pesos each. These citizens were:

1. Antonio de Figueroa*
2. Juan Adrián F. Cornejo*
3. Francisco de Toledo Pimental*
4. Fernando de Torres*
5. Francisco G. de San Millán*
6. Lucas de Allende
7. Félix Arias Rengel*
8. José Antonio F. Cornejo*

[1]This information was found in Cornejo, *Historia* . . . p. 13.
*Indicates a direct connection to the kinship elite.

SAMPLE OF THE MEMBERS OF A COLONIAL CABILDO[1]

1795—

1. Nicolás Isamendi
2. Antonio de Figueroa*
3. Sinforosa J. de Rioja
4. Miguel Francisco Gómez
5. Apolinar Figueroa*
6. Mateo Gómez Zorrilla
7. Pedro López

[1]This information was found in Cornejo, *Apuntes* . . . pp. 596-97.
*Indicates membership in the kinship elite.

APPENDIX D

THE MILITARY POWER OF THE KINSHIP ELITE

LEADERS OF GAUCHO RESISTANCE TO THE INVASION OF PEZUELA IN 1814 AND THEIR RELATIONSHIP TO THE FAMILY STRUCTURE[1]

General commanders:

Pedro José Saravia	SGCt
Martín Güemes	GCFts
Apolinar Saravia	SGCt
José Antonio Cornejo	CFTGS
Pablo Latorre	TS
Toribio Tedin	
Pedro Ferreyra	
Satúrnino Saravia	SCftg
Luis Burla	ST
Pedro Zavala	
José Francisco Gorriti	GFCt
José Gabino Sarbina	
José María Lahora	
Antonio Viscara	
Francisco María Cornejo	CGFTs
Pablo de Latorre	TS
José Francisco Tineo	GSc
José Eustaquio Moldes	
Santiago Figueroa	FCGTs
Elias de Iriarte	g
Francisco Solano Pérez	
Pedro Antonio Arrieta	
Narciso Figueroa	FCGTs
José Gregorio Arrieta	
Fernando Aramburu	
Juan Manuel de Ojeda	
Juan Francisco de Zamudio	
José Fernández	Fc
Manuel Gómez	
Total 29	15

[1]This list was obtained from Cornejo, *Historia* . . . pp. 103-106.

RANKING MILITARY COMMANDERS OF THE PROVINCE OF SALTA IN 1819 AND THEIR RELATIONSHIP TO THE FAMILY STRUCTURE[1]

D. Bartolomé de la Corte, Lt. Governor of Jujuy	GCfs
D. Francisco Pérez de Uriondo, Lt. Governor of Tarija	

D. Eusebio M. Mollinedo, Ayudante de Gobierno .... TF
Dr. Francisco Claudio Castro, Asesor de Gobierno
D. José M. Lahora, Ayudante Mayor de Plaza
D. Pedro José Zavala, Mayor de Plaza
D. Apolinar Saravia, Jefe del Estado Mayor .... SGCt
D. Vicente Torino, Director de la Maestranza de Armas
D. Narciso Núñez, Comandante de artillería
D. Mariano Pino, Comandante de artillería
D. José Manuel Vaca, Director de la Fábrica de pólvora
Dr. Antonio Castellanos, Físico de la tropa .... FCtgs
D. José Mateo Fernández, Administrador del Hospital .... F
D. Manuel Morales, Ayudante de Campo
D. Pedro A. Ceballos, Ministro Contador .... FGct
Dr. Pedro Buitrago, Fiscal interino de Hacienda
Mariano Zavala, commander of a division of gauchos
Francisco Velarde, commander of a division of gauchos .... Gcf
Francisco María Cornejo, commander of a division of gauchos .... GCFTs
Luis Burla, commander of a division of gauchos .... ST
Sinforoso Morales, commander of a division of gauchos
Ángel M. Zerda, commander of a division of gauchos .... g
D. Juan Antonio Rojas, Commander of the Vanguard
D. Francisco Salas, Captain de Granaderos a caballo
Col. José Antonio Cornejo, Commander of the Partidarios .... CFTGS

Thus the family structure held these positions: Lt. Governor of Jujuy; Chief of Staff; Adjutant of the government; Surgeon General; Ranking Medical Officer; Commands of four out of six divisions of gauchos; General command of the frontier.

[1]This information was obtained from Cornejo, *Historia* . . . pp. 261-62.

APPENDIX E

MISCELLANEOUS INFORMATION

REPRESENTATION OF THE CABILDO AND THE PROVINCE OF SALTA IN THE NATIONAL ASSEMBLIES[1]

Assembly of 1810—Francisco Gurrachaga
Assembly of 1812—Francisco Gurrachaga
Assembly of 1813—José Moldes
Congress of Tucumán of 1816—Mariano Boedo
                                José Ignacio Gorriti
                                José Moldes
Congress of Tucumán of 1819—Marcos Salomé Zorrilla
                                Mateo Saravia
Legislature of the United Provinces of 1819—
        Representatives—Marcos Salomé Zorrilla
                        Pedro Antonio Velasco
                        Guillermo de Ormaechea
        Senators—Manuel Antonio Castro
                 José Ignacio Gorriti
Congress of Córdoba of 1820—Juan de la Cruz Monge y Orteaga
                                Manuel Antonio Castro

[1]This information was obtained from Cornejo, *Apuntes* . . . pp. 619-20.

A SAMPLE OF A FORCED LEVY ON THE SPANISH MERCHANTS—OCTOBER 18, 1813[1]
(In Pesos)

D. Lino de Rosales	2,000
D. Atansio Villar	200
D. Tomás del Campo	200
D. Juan Nadal y Guarda	1,500
D. José Rincón	1,000
D. Jaime Nadal	1,500
D. Domingo Cardo	220
D. Pablo Lesser	200
D. Cipriano Enjo	200
D. Miguel Francisco Gómez	500
D. Francisco Valdés	200
D. Francisco García	200
D. Santiago Cerdán	200
D. Francisco Tejada	1,000
D. Marcos Beeche	500
D. Pedro José de Ibazeta	2,000
D. José de Uriburu	2,000
D. Matías Gómez Linares	500

D. José Antonio Echevarría 2,000
D. Manuel Antonio Tejada 500
D. Santiago Maseyra 300
D. Juan Quincot 100
D. Antonio Águila 1,500
D. Francisco Grana 1,300
D. Francisco Nevares 300
D. Bernabé Fernández 50

[1]Reproduced from Cornejo, *Historia* . . . pp. 97-98.

CAREER OF JOSÉ ANTONIO CORNEJO[1]

December 14, 1810............	The Provisional Junta named him Lt. Colonel in the patriot army.
November 5, 1812............	Belgrano promoted him to colonel of the Regiment of Dragoons in Salta.
May 22, 1813.................	He was appointed commandant of the Fronteras district.
June 8, 1814.................	Posadas recalled him to his former position in the militia of Salta. His rank was colonel.
August 7, 1814................	He was appointed provisional military governor of Salta.
April 2, 1814.................	He was again appointed provisional military governor of Salta.
1815-1818	He was in command of the gaucho forces of the Fronteras region.
September 2, 1818............	Pueyrredón named him colonel of the cavalry.
August 15, 1821...............	He was given the rank of colonel in the proposed expeditionary force to Upper Peru.
May 24, 1821.................	The cabildo of Salta named him military commander of the province.
June 17, 1821.................	Güemes died and Cornejo assumed command of the resistance.
August 9, 1821................	José Antonio Cornejo was elected Governor of the province of Salta.

[1]This information was obtained from Cornejo, *Apuntes* . . . pp. 200-207.

OCCUPATIONS OF INDIVIDUALS IN AND AROUND SALTA[1]

Merchants

Miguel Aráoz.	León Urteaga
Guillermo Ormaechea	José María Nadal
Lorenzo Olmos	Teodoro López
Santiago López	José Gurrachaga
Manuel Castañeda	Pedro Pablo Arias
Maximiliano López	Baltazar Usandivares
Inocencio Torino	Camilo Velarde
Joaquín Achaval	Vicente de Zenarruza
	José Hilario Carol

Lawyers
Juan Manuel Güemes
Manuel Antonio de Castro
Pedro A. Arias Velásquez
Mariano Boedo
Francisco Claudio Castro

Estancieros
Pedro José Saravia
Santiago Figueroa
Narciso Figueroa
Apolinar Figueroa
Fructuoso Figueroa
José Antonio Cornejo
Francisco María Cornejo

Satúrnino Saravia
Apolinar Saravia
Pablo Latorre
Toribio Tedin
Pedro Ferreyra
Pedro Zavala
Luis Burla
José Gabino Sarbina
José Fernández
Vicente Toledo

Bolivian Rebels in Salta
Juan de la Cruz Monge y Orteaga
Manuel de Ulloa
Mariano José de Ulloa

[1]This information was compiled from scattered data in Cornejo, *Historia* . . .

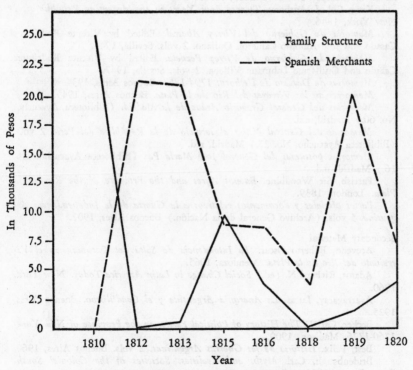

Voluntary Contributions and Taxes That Financed the
Activities of Salta From 1810 to 1820

BIBLIOGRAPHY

Manuscript Sources
  Archivo General de la Provincia de Salta. Salta, Argentina.

Printed Documents, Collections, Memorias, etc.
  Actas del Cabildo: Documentos Tucumanos. Edited by Manuel L. Borda. 2 vols. Tucumán, 1939.
  Acuerdos del Extinguido Cabildo de Buenos Aires. 48 vols. (Archivo General de la Nación, Series 1-4.) Buenos Aires, 1907-1934.
  Documentos del Archivo de Belgrano: Museo Mitre. 6 vols. Buenos Aires, 1914-1916.
  Documentos del Archivo de San Martín. 12 vols. Buenos Aires, 1910-1911.
  Documentos para la Historia Argentina. Buenos Aires, 1913-.
  Documentos para la Historia de Libertador General San Martín. 8 vols. Buenos Aires, 1944-1945.
  Head, Captain F. B. *Rough Notes Taken During Some Rapid Journeys Across the Pampas.* 2nd ed. London, 1826.
  King, Col. J. Anthony. *Twenty Four Years in the Argentine Republic . . .* New York, 1846.
  Memoria de Gobierno del Virrey Abascal. Edited by Vicente Rodríguez Casado and José Antonio Calderón Quijano. 2 vols. Sevilla, 1944.
  Memoria de Gobierno de Virrey Pezuela. Edited by Vicente Rodríguez Casado and Guillermo Lohmann Villena. 2 vols. Sevilla, 1947.
  Memorias de Dámaso de Uriburu: 1794-1857. Buenos Aires, 1934.
  Memorias de los Virreyes del Río de la Plata. Buenos Aires, 1945.
  Memorias del General Gregorio Aráoz de la Madrid. (Biblioteca Ayacucho, No. 60.) Madrid, n.d.
  Memorias del General Miller al servicio de la República del Peru. 2 vols. (Biblioteca Ayacucho, No. 27.) Madrid, n.d.
  Memorias póstumas del General José María Paz (Biblioteca Ayacucho, No. 16.) Madrid, n.d.
  Parrish, Sir Woodbine. *Buenos Ayres and the Province of the Río de la Plata.* London, 1839.
  Partes oficiales y documentos relativos a la Guerra de la Independencia Argentina. 5 vols. (Archivo General de la Nación.) Buenos Aires, 1902.

Secondary Material
  Acevedo, Edberto Oscar. *La Intendencia de Salta del Tucumán en el Virreinato del Río de la Plata.* Mendoza, 1965.
  Adams, Richard N. (ed.) *Social Change in Latin America Today.* New York, 1960.
  Ayarragaray, Lucas, *La Anarquía Argentina y el Caudillismo.* Buenos Aires, 1925.
  Becker, Carl L. *The History of Political Parties in the Province of New York, 1760-1776.* Madison, 1909.
  Best, Félix. *Historia de las Guerras Argentinas.* 2 vols. Buenos Aires, 1960.
  Bridenbaugh, Carl. *Myths and Realities: Societies of the Colonial South.* Baton Rouge, 1952.
  Cornejo, Atilio. *Apuntes Históricos sobre Salta.* Buenos Aires, 1937.
  ———. *Historia de Güemes,* Buenos Aires, 1946.

72

Freyre, Gilberto. *The Masters and Slaves.* New York, 1946.

Frías, Bernardo. *Historia de General D. Martín Güemes y de la Provincia de Salta de 1810 a 1832.* 3 vols. Salta, 1902.

Gandia, Enrique de. *Historia de la república Argentina en el siglo XIX.* Buenos Aires, 1940.

Haring, Clarence H. *The Spanish Empire in America.* New York, 1947.

Heath, Dwight B., and Richard N. Adams. *Contemporary Cultures and Societies of Latin America.* New York, 1965.

James, Preston. *Latin America.* Rev. ed. New York, 1951.

Kirkpatrick, Frederick A. *A History of the Argentine Republic.* Cambridge, 1931.

Labaree, Leonard W. *Conservatism in Early American History.* New York, 1948.

Levene, Ricardo. *A History of Argentina.* (The Inter-American Historical Series.) Edited and translated by James A. Robertson. Chapel Hill, 1937.

————. *Historia de la Nación Argentina.* 10 vols. Buenos Aires, 1945.

Levillier, Roberto. *Los origenes de Tucumán.* Buenos Aires, 1945.

López, Vicente. *Historia de la República Argentina.* 10 vols. Buenos Aires, 1913.

Mitre, Bartolomé. *Estudios Históricos sobre la Revolución Argentina: Belgrano y Güemes.* Buenos Aires, 1864.

————. *Historia de Belgrano y de la Independencia Argentina.* 3 vols. Buenos Aires, 1858.

————. *Historia de San Martin. . . .* 4 vols. Buenos Aires, 1890.

Nichols, Madaline W. *The Gaucho.* Durham, 1942.

Ots Capedequí, José María. *Manual de Historia del derecho en las Indias y del derecho propiamente indiano.* Buenos Aires, 1945.

————. *El Estado español en las Indias.* Mexico: D.F., 1965.

Puiggros, Rodolfo. *Los Caudillos de la Revolución de Mayo.* Buenos Aires, 1942.

Razori, Ámilcar. *Historia de la cuidad Argentina.* 3 vols. Buenos Aires, 1945.

Revista de la Biblioteca Nacional. Buenos Aires, 1938.

Sánchez de Bustamente, Teófilo. *Biográficos históricos de Jujuy.* Tucumán, 1957.

Sierra, Vicente. *Historia de la Argentina.* 4 vols. Buenos Aires, 1958-1960.

Smith, Page. *The Historian and History.* New York, 1964.

Solá, Miguel. *Erección y Abolición del Cabildo de Salta.* Buenos Aires, 1936.

White, John W. *Argentina: The Life Story of a Nation.* New York, 1942.

Zinny, Antonio. (ed.) *Gaceta de Buenos Aires: desde 1810 hasta 1820.* Buenos Aires, 1875.

————. *Historia de las gobernadores de las provincias Argentinas.* 5 vols. Buenos Aires. 1916-1921.

Index

A

Abascal, Fernando de, 27
Agrarian Reform Law, 30, 49
Aguirre family, 17
Alberru, Francisco Antonio, 45-46
Alvarado family, 17
Alvarado, Ángel, 19
Alvarado, Juan Francisco, 19
Alvarado, Severo de, 19, 40
Álvarez, Thomás, 25
Alvear, Carlos, 7, 8, 24, 44
Ancieta family, 17
Aramburu family, 5
Aráoz family, 17
Aráoz, Bernabé, 7, 21, 34-36
Aráoz, Francisco, 18, 26
Aráoz, Miguel F., 45
Archondo, Luis, 36
Arenales family, 17
Arenales, Álvarez de, 18
Arenales, Mercedes, 18
Arias family, 17, 21
Arias, Álejo, 45, 47
Arias, Gaspar, 19
Arias, Grimensa, 18
Arias, Juan P., 18
Arias, Manuel Eduardo, 28
Arias, Pedro Pablo, 18, 46-48
Arias Rengel, Nicolás, 18
Arias Velásquez, Dr. Pedro, 18, 25-26, 48
Army of the North, 4, 7, 20, 25-27
Assembly of Castañanes, 31
Assembly of Deputies, 26, 47
Ayohuma, 5, 9, 42

B

Balcarce, Antonio G., 3-4, 9, 41
Banda Oriental, 51
Belgrano, Manuel, 4-6, 8-10, 15-17, 30, 34, 42
Boedo family, 17
Boedo, José Francisco, 18
Boedo, Mariano, 19, 26-27, 47-48
Boedo, Ventura, 18-19
Buenos Aires, 3-4, 7-10, 13, 16, 18-21, 24-25, 27, 31, 34, 41, 42
Bulwark of the North, 6
Burla family, 17
Burla Inés, 18
Burla, José, 18
Burla, Luis, 6, 29, 42, 51
Bustos, Juan Bautista, 34

C

Cabildo, v, 18, 19, 24, 25, 45-47
Cabildo abierto, 2
Campo Santo, 14
Campos, Pedro José, 32
Castellanos family, 17
Castellanos, Dr. Antonio, 36
Castellanos, Juan José, 48
Castellanos, Teresa, 46
Castelli, Juan José, 3, 4, 8, 9
Castro family, 5
Castro, Dr. Manuel Antonio de, 32, 34
Catamarca, 34
Ceballos family, 17
Ceballos, Pedro A., 46
Cerrillo, Ángela, 40
Charcas, Archbishop of, 3
Chiclana, Feliciano, 3, 5, 13, 15
Cochabamba, 4
Compadrazgo, vi
Congress of Tucumán, 27, 47, 48
Constitutional Assembly of 1816, 27
Córdoba, 3, 8, 41; Congress of, 34
Cornejo, Atilio, vi
Cornejo family, Economic position, 14-20; Military influence, 14-15, 20; Political power, 18-19, 45-48; Connections to related families, 17
Cornejo, Antonio F., 16
Cornejo, Cornelia, 16
Cornejo, Francisco María, 14
Cornejo, Gabino, 46-47
Cornejo, Gregorio A., 16
Cornejo, José Antonio, 3, 14, 16-19, 36, 37, 42, 48, 50, 51
Cornejo, Juan Adrián F., 14, 16, 41, 45
Cornejo, Juan José, 18
Cornejo, Juan N., 46
Cornejo, Magdalena, 16, 19, 46
Cornejo, María, 17
Cornejo, María Antonia, 19, 45, 46
Cornejo, María Ignacia, 16
Cornejo, María Mercedes, 16
Cornejo, Tiburcio, 18, 19
Cornejo y la Corte, María Ignacia Fernández, 41

74

Martín Güemes:
TYRANT OR TOOL?

*Other books in the series from
Texas Christian University Press*

No. 1

Fine Texas Horses, Their
Pedigrees and Performance, 1830-1845
by Malcolm D. McLean

No. 2

Maria Edgeworth The Novelist
by James Newcomer

TEXAS CHRISTIAN UNIVERSITY PRESS, FORT WORTH